Klaus Paysan

AQUARIUM FISH
from Around the World

Lerner Publications Company
Minneapolis, Minnesota

The Library of Congress cataloged the original printing of this title as follows:

Paysan, Klaus.
    Aquarium fish from around the world. [Photos and text by] Klaus Paysan. [Sketches by Angela Paysan. English translation by Susan W. Dickinson] Minneapolis, Lerner Publications Co. [1970, c1967]
    106 p. col. illus. 22 cm.
    Describes briefly the feeding, mating habits, and general characteristics of fifty aquarium fish. Includes a photograph of each specimen.
    1. Aquarium fishes—Juvenile literature. 2. Aquarium fishes—Pictorial works. [1. Aquarium fishes. 2. Fishes] I. Paysan, Angela, illus. II. Title.

SF457.P3813 1970	639'.34	73-102892
ISBN 0-8225-0561-4		MARC
		AC

A NATURE AND MAN BOOK

First published in the United States 1970 by Lerner Publications Company, Minneapolis, Minnesota. All English language rights reserved.
Copyright © MCMLXVII by Deutsche Verlags-Anstalt, Stuttgart, Germany.

International Standard Book Number: 0-8225-0561-4
Library of Congress Catalog Card Number: 73-102892

Manufactured in the United States of America

3 4 5 6 7 8 9 10 92 91 90 89 88 87 86 85 84 83

CONTENTS

- 8 Goldfish
- 10 Comet
- 12 Common Veiltail
- 14 Stargazer
- 16 Golden Orfe
- 18 Three-spined Stickleback
- 20 Guppy
- 22 Green Swordtail
- 24 Red Swordtail
- 26 Platy
- 28 Black Molly
- 30 Sailfin Molly
- 32 Blue Fundulus
- 34 Bertholdi's Aphyosemion
- 36 Sparkling Panchax
- 38 Zebra Danio
- 40 Pearl Danio
- 42 Sumatra or Tiger Barb
- 44 Golden Barb
- 46 Rosy Barb
- 48 Harlequin Fish
- 50 Sucking Gyrinocheilus
- 52 Clown Loach
- 54 Red-tailed Black Shark
- 56 Bronze Corydoras or Catfish
- 58 Glass Catfish or Ghost Fish
- 60 Indian Glass Fish
- 62 Pumpkinseed
- 64 Ramirezi's Dwarf Cichlid
- 66 Peacock or Dwarf Rainbow Cichlid
- 68 Blue or Texas Cichlid
- 70 Mother-of-Pearl Cichlid
- 72 Banded Cichlid
- 74 Discus or Pompadour
- 76 Angel Fish
- 78 Paradise Fish
- 80 Siamese Fighting Fish
- 82 Three-spot Gourami
- 84 Lace Gourami
- 86 Dwarf Gourami
- 88 Diagonal Swimmer or Penguin Fish
- 90 Serpae Tetra
- 92 Flame Fish or Flame Tetra
- 94 X-ray Fish
- 96 Ornate or Rosy Tetra
- 98 Glowlight Tetra
- 100 Neon Tetra
- 102 Cardinal Tetra
- 104 Red-nosed Tetra
- 106 Congo Tetra

Introduction

The care of fish is a constant source of pleasure for many people. Man can give small fish a home that is very similar to their natural home in lakes, streams, rivers, and oceans. An aquarium is the best place to keep fish away from their natural environment. The size of an aquarium might seem small in comparison to a lake or stream, but the actual living areas of fish are very limited. Even a large fish like a trout has a living area in his stream that is very small. As a child I often visited a stickleback fish in a woodland stream. It stayed in the same small area from year to year, and always built its nest and reared its young in the same place.

If an aquarium is very small, however, it is not able to provide fish with the healthy biological climate necessary for their full development. An aquarium tank should contain from 10 to 13 gallons of water, for only then do the fish have enough room to set invisible boundaries to their areas. The plant life in the tank should be as similar as possible to the plant life in a fish's natural home because it is accustomed to living in those particular water conditions. Any change in the conditions could bring about very unfortunate results. Good ventilation of aquarium water is also a necessity if there is to be enough oxygen in the tank for the fish to breathe. If the tank is not overcrowded with fish and has enough water surface, it should provide an adequate supply of oxygen. Plants in an aquarium will also add to the oxygen supply because they absorb some of the carbon dioxide given off by the fish and in return give off oxygen. The water in the tank can be kept clean and clear with a filter. A well-planned aquarium kept at the correct temperature by thermostatic heating and lit by a neon light can easily be left unattended for six months. An occasional replacement of the water lost by evaporation might be necessary until it is time to take out a large amount of the water and replace it with fresh water.

Feeding the fish is no longer a problem for the aquarist. It may be difficult for people living in cities to find ponds filled with water fleas, but every good pet shop has a large selection of different fresh fish foods. Water fleas, cyclops, and red and black mosquito eggs can almost always be found in shops that handle fish and aquarium equipment. If food cannot be supplied fresh, it is still possible to buy frozen fish food. This can be thrown into the aquarium with the surrounding packing ice; the fish will wait for the food to thaw out and then gobble it up. Dried food can also be bought in many varieties. With so many different forms of fish food available, it should be possible to provide the correct diet required by any kind of fish. The sensitive and rare varieties of fish need a varied diet. The more common, easily kept varieties of fish will also appreciate a diet of food that has nutritional value and a variety of colors.

Each aquarist is able to choose the particular kinds of fish he wishes to keep in his aquarium. Some people only like aquariums where they can keep a pair or group of one kind of fish with the plants from their natural settings. Others like a variety of fish and prefer to keep a mixed aquarium with several different kinds of plants and fish.

A combination of fish varieties can lend special charm to an aquarium. Different species of fish prefer to stay in particular areas of the aquarium, but each species should have sufficient room in its area to develop freely. Let us look at one example of a typical mixed aquarium. Near the bottom of this aquarium catfish are swimming slowly around, and if you look closely, you can see loaches hiding in holes in trees or circling close to the bottom. Cichlids and glass fish can be seen swimming around in a thicket of plants. A large group of tetras and x-ray fish occupy the middle area of the aquarium, and they form a beautiful contrast of colors. Paradise fish are swimming playfully back and forth near the surface of the water, dwarf gouramis are busily building their nests, and the fighting fish are swimming back and forth with their colorful fins outspread. A sucking gyrinocheilus is eagerly cleaning up all the algae in the aquarium. An Indian water fern with its feathery light green leaves contrasts with a dark green Amazon sword plant. Fine-leaved plants are planted in groups, and the other small plants form a jungle of plant life on the bottom. The plants and the root of a tree placed in a corner offer good hiding places for the fish.

The advanced aquarist not only likes to keep beautiful fish but also concerns himself with the breeding of difficult species. Anyone with an aquarium will find that it becomes an endless source of observation and entertainment. He can watch his fish as they go through their change of color during mating time, follow strict ceremonies during mating and egg laying, and care for their young. He can then work with the actual problems of keeping fish. Through such research he might be able to discover new information about the behavior of the more familiar varieties of fish, as well as the behavior of new imports.

Goldfish

This golden species of fish was bred by the Chinese from the plain blue-brown carp that is sometimes called the crucian carp. The breeding and raising of goldfish began more than a thousand years ago, and since that time many more goldfish varieties have been discovered. In the 17th century goldfish were first brought to Europe, where they became a favorite of fish lovers. Today the goldfish is one of the most widely kept species in the cold water aquarium. It is easily raised, but it must not be kept in too small a container. It only shows off its most beautiful colors and swimming antics in a large, well-ventilated aquarium which has an abundant plant life. The goldfish is not particular about water temperature, but as the water becomes colder it becomes lazier. In winter goldfish should be kept in water temperatures of 50°F.

The scientific name for the goldfish is *Carassius auratus*. It can grow to 8 inches long and eats plants, and dried and living food.

Water temperature: 39.2° to 68°F.

Comet

The comet fish is a member of the carp family and can be traced to a form of the veiltail species of goldfish. Carps are very fertile and lay more than 10,000 eggs at once. Because of this, the Chinese were able to select from many mutations and variations of the carp in their breeding experiments. They have been able to produce goldfish and comets in many varieties of color from a brass color to a golden red, to flesh-colored and white. Some goldfish have an interesting checked coloring which is occasionally combined with a very long fin. It is interesting to watch the young comets change color. They are black at first and do not change to their beautiful gold coloring until after the first 8 to 12 months. Comets can live in a wide range of temperatures and can be easily kept in an aquarium.

Carassius auratus originated in China. It will grow up to 12 inches long and eats plants and dried food.

Water temperature: 39.2° to 68°F.

Common Veiltail

The Chinese proved their skill in fish breeding when they developed the veiltail fish from the goldfish. Veiltails are beautiful in form, fins, and coloring, and are thought by many aquarists to be some of the best examples of fish breeding. They can be easily kept in a well-planted aquarium. In Asia the veiltail is kept in flat porcelain or wooden containers because the beauty of its many fins can best be appreciated when seen from above. Its fat, overfull belly is also not as noticeable from above as when seen from another angle. From a top view the entire fish seems to consist of elegant, floating fins. There are many varieties of veiltail, such as the checked, dappled, black, and scaleless veiltails. These finer, higher breeds of goldfish are more difficult to keep in an aquarium because they require warmer water temperatures. Even in winter the water temperature should not be allowed to drop below 59°F.

Carassius auratus eats plants and dried food.

Water temperature: 59° to 89.6°F.

Stargazer

The numerous breeds of goldfish show that fish can appear in many different forms. Many varieties of fish in addition to the goldfish are bred from the carp species. The carp's great fertility gives an experienced aquarist the opportunity to experiment in breeding many varieties. As you can see from some of the fish pictured in this book, almost every extreme of breeding is possible. Different parent fish can be bred and crossed, and further breeding and sorting of types will result in new and interesting fish. The stargazer is an unusual form of goldfish which was developed through this method of crossbreeding.

Carassius auratus comes from China. It eats plants and dried food.

Water temperature: 68° to 89.6°F.

Golden Orfe

This is a golden variation of the ide fish which lives in the rivers and lakes of Europe. Since it grows very slowly and eats all kinds of food, the golden orfe is a suitable inhabitant for a beginner's unheated aquarium. When the fish become too large for the aquarium they can easily be put in their natural homes of ponds or lakes. The golden orfe's breeding season extends from April to June, and it lays its eggs on stones and plants. The best plants for its aquarium home are those which do not die in winter. The golden orfe is especially beautiful when swimming in a shoal, or group. The wild variety of golden orfe has dark coloring on its back and a silver-gray color on its sides.

Idus Idus grows up to 20 inches long and eats all kinds of food.

Water temperature: 41° to 68°F.

Three-spined Stickleback

The stickleback is a modestly colored fish, but during mating time the male's colors turn as gay as those of the most colorful tropical fish. At the beginning of the breeding season the male stickleback makes a depression on the sandy bottom of a lake. With strands of moss and plants he builds a round nest with a large entrance and a small exit. When he has finished the nest he returns to the shoal in search of females and chases several of them into his nest. When they lay their eggs he enters the nest and fertilizes them. A male stickleback may have as many as 10 mates; he stops mating only when his nest is full of eggs. He then guards the nest and fans fresh water over the eggs with his breast fin. He chases away everything that comes too near the nest with threatening, angry bites. When the young fish hatch and try to leave the nest he chases them back. As they grow older the young can leave the nest with the male, but they must return to the nest to spend the night.

Gasterosteus aculeatus comes from Europe. It grows to 3 or 4 inches long and eats living food.

Water temperature: 41° to 68°F.

Guppy

This small fish is sometimes called "million fish" because, like other members of the carp family, it produces young very often. But instead of laying eggs, the guppy produces its young alive. Every three weeks a healthy female guppy can produce up to 100 young. The guppy has a fondness for mosquito eggs and is a valuable helper to the malaria fighters because it helps to keep the malaria-carrying mosquitoes from multiplying. Guppies are put into even the smallest lakes for that purpose. The guppy can be kept in unheated room aquariums but it prefers warmer water temperatures. The larger females are always a yellow-gray color, but the guppy males vary a great deal in color depending on their living area. This is why it has been possible to breed guppies with many different colors and fin formations. Flagtail guppies, spade tails, pin tails, pointed tails, round tails, lyre tails, veiltails, top swords, bottom swords, and double swords are some of the most important varieties.

Lebistes reticulatus comes from Central and South America. It grows up to 2 inches long and eats plants, and dried and living food.

Water temperature: 64.4° to 77°F.

Green Swordtail

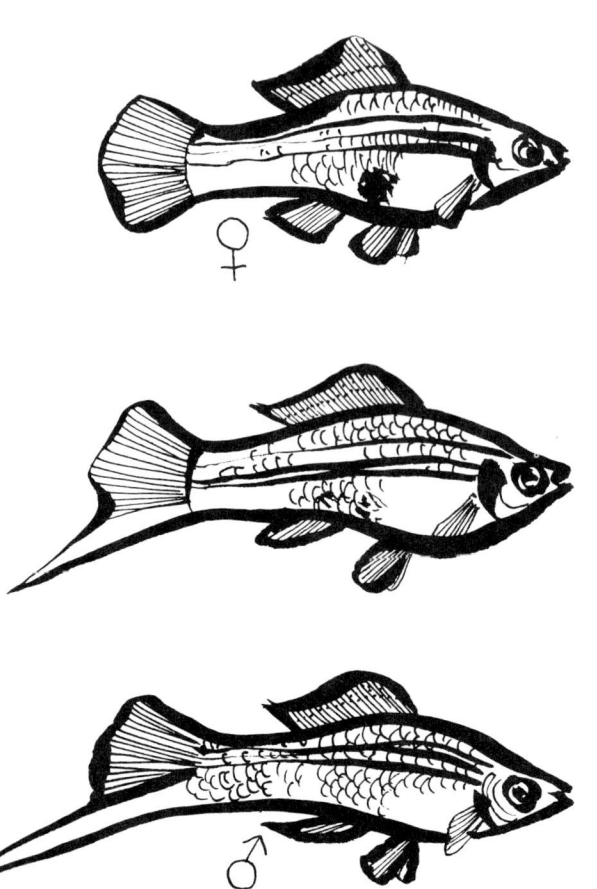

Although the male and female swordtails resemble each other in color, they do not resemble each other in form. The males grow to a greater length than the females, and the lower part of the male's tail fin lengthens to form a long sword. The females are heavier and larger than the males. Occasionally these fish may reverse sexes — a male will change into a female and a female into a male. When a female green swordtail changes to a male, its tail fin grows into a sword, the pregnancy mark under the tail fin disappears, and the body becomes longer. This change results from an alteration or displacement of hormones. As the female grows older, fewer female sex hormones are produced and the male sex hormones become stronger and dominant. The new hormone grouping regulates behavior and body shape. The sex change is a change in only the outward physical features of the fish. When a swordtail goes through such a change it is no longer able to reproduce.

Xiphophorus helleri comes from Central America. It grows up to 4 inches long and eats plants, and dried and living food.

Water temperature: 64.4° to 73.4°F.

Red Swordtail

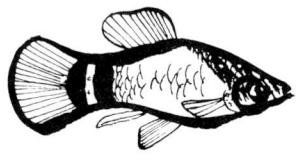

Because of their great fertility, live-bearing carp species are favorite breeding and crossing fish. The red swordtail resulted from a cross between the red platy and the green swordtail. Its many shades of color make this fish a welcome addition to the aquarium. Such specially reared species are more sensitive to water temperature than fish that are not specially bred and should be kept in warmer temperatures of water. All these carp varieties eat dried food, but they occasionally need varieties of fresh vegetables or live animal food to aid their development. They also need plant material for food, and are a great help in the aquarium because they eat plant remains and algae. Our sketch shows varieties of platys and swordtails: at the top is a female red swordtail, and below from the left are the yellow platy, wagtail platy, and blue platy.

Xiphophorus helleri X Xiphophorus maculatus (green swordtail crossed with red platy) grows up to 4 inches long and eats plants, and dried and living food.

Water temperature: 68° to 78.8°F.

Platy

Like the swordtail and the guppy, the platy belongs to the family of live-bearing carp. It can be found in many varieties of shape and color. The females of this species can easily be recognized by a pregnancy mark under the tail fin. The females are usually larger than the males, but the males are more colorful. The male of the platy species has many mates. This is probably because the females can store many seeds from one fertilization and give birth to several series of young after only one mating. These fish live naturally in well-vegetated waters and should be kept in well-planted aquariums.

Xiphophorus (Platypoecilus) variatus comes from Mexico. It grows up to 3 inches long and eats plants, and dried and living food.

Water temperature: 64.4° to 77°F.

Black Molly

The black molly is a form of the pointed-nosed carp that comes from the coastal regions of Central America. In its original state the fish is not very unusual in color, but its color can be changed greatly through breeding. Black mollies are very sensitive to changes in water temperature and must be kept warm. They like aquariums that are well lighted and abundantly planted. They can be kept in fresh water, but seem to prefer a touch of sea salt added to the water. Like all fish of this species, black mollies eat dried food and need plenty of plant food for their well-being. This can be given to them in the form of soaked lettuce leaves laid in the water of the aquarium. Black mollies also can be bred from other varieties of carp besides the pointed nose variety and have many different shapes of fins.

Mollienisia sphenops grows up to 3 inches long.

Water temperature: 75.2° to 82.4°F.

Sailfin Molly

This beautiful fish will make its home in both fresh water and salt water. In aquariums it is usually kept in fresh water, but it seems to be more comfortable if a bit of salt is added to the water. The male has a sail-shaped dorsal (back) fin which it raises during courtship. One unexplained peculiarity of the sailfin molly is that the large dorsal fin is only completely formed when the fish is reared in an open pool. When it is reared in an aquarium it develops only a small dorsal fin. Water-plant gardeners like to keep the sailfin molly in their plant pools because these fish have large appetites and will eat any dead leaves floating in the water. The males are very lively and keep the aquarium water moving with their play and constant chase of the females.

Mollienisia velifera comes from Mexico. It grows up to 4 inches long and eats plants, and dried and living food.

Water temperature: 75.2° to 82.4°F.

Blue Fundulus

The natural home of the blue fundulus is East Africa, where the weather alternates between rainy seasons and long dry periods. Because of this the fish adapts easily to changes in its living conditions. Its eggs can survive dry periods in the dust and the young fish will hatch from them as soon as the rain falls. The blue fundulus may even be found living in puddles. If the puddle dries up the parents die but the eggs survive. Young fish of this variety can also be found in tire tracks filled with water during the rainy season. The young fish grow quickly and are able to reproduce after three to four weeks. These seasonal fish are so well adjusted to their short life span in their natural habitat that they do not live in an aquarium for much more than a year. On the other hand, if they are well fed they are continually active and always ready to display their courting colors. Unfortunately, it is difficult to distinguish between the varieties of females of this species when they are alive, and because of this, undesired results often arise from cross breeding.

Nothobranchius guentheri grows to 3½ inches long and eats dried and living food.

Water temperature: **68° to 77°F.**

34 Bertholdi's Aphyosemion

Every year explorers searching in the tropics for new aquarium fish find strange and interesting varieties and sub-varieties. New, fantastically colored varieties of aphyosemion are constantly appearing. The aphyosemion in our picture was only discovered a few years ago in West Africa and is still often sold in shops under the wrong name, usually cap lopez. The color of the male of this variety of aphyosemion depends on its mood and can vary from steel blue to emerald green. If it feels unwell its color fades to a light brown beige. The female of this variety is light brown with a few red spots and can easily be confused with females of other aphyosemion species. She lays her eggs on fine-leaved plants. Like the eggs of the blue fundulus, the eggs of the aphyosemion can survive dry periods without water.

Aphiosemium bertholdi comes from Sierra Leone in West Africa. It grows up to 2½ inches long and eats both dried and living food.

Water temperature: 71.6° to 75.2°F.

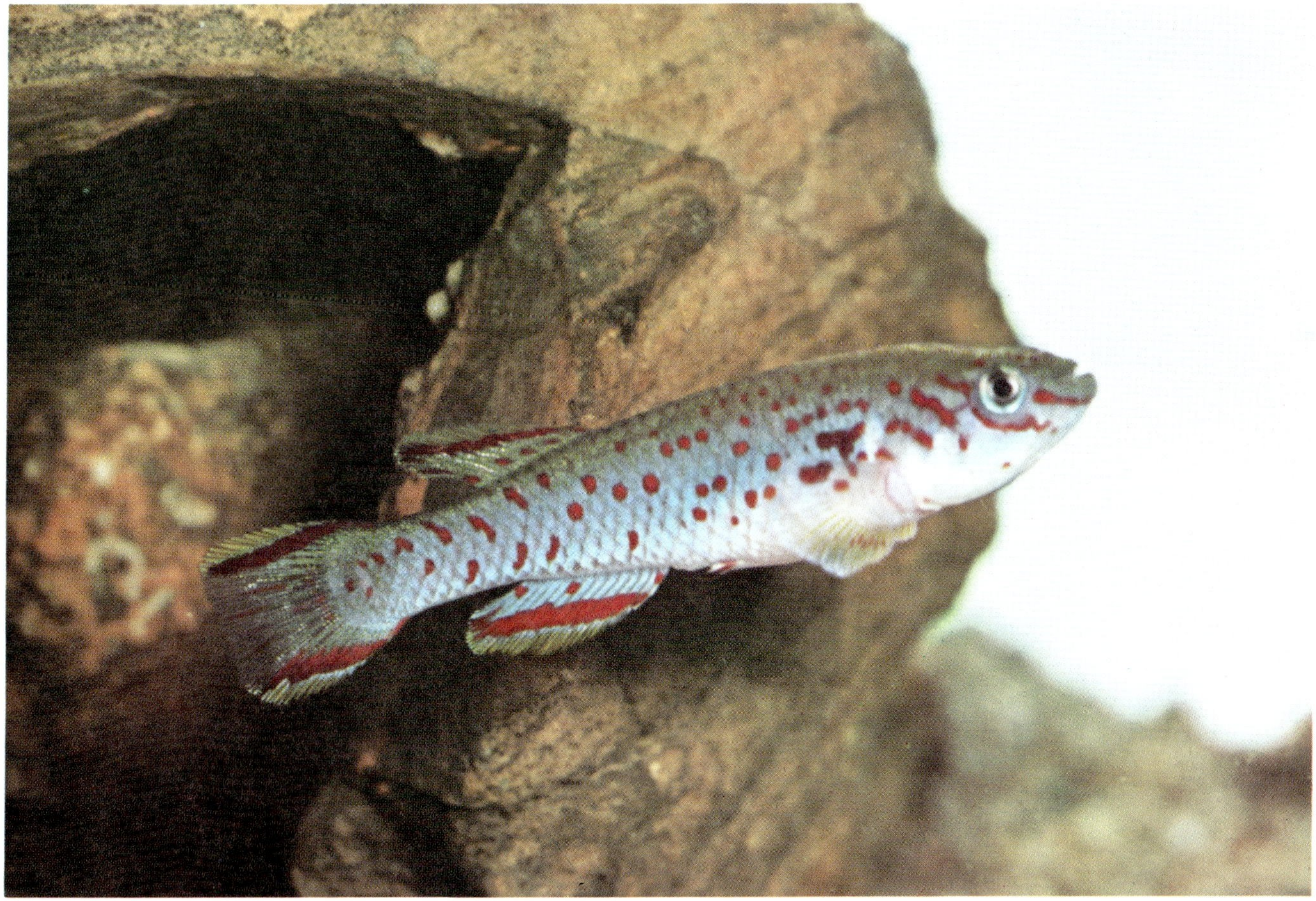

Sparkling Panchax

The sparkling panchax lives along the bank areas of rivers and streams and swims just under the surface of the water. The shape of its body is adapted to this behavior; the back of the fish forms a straight line which lies directly along the water surface. There is a shiny spot on the top of its head which is thought to attract insects, since insects and smaller fish are its main sources of food. It also loves to eat mosquito eggs and is highly valued in India because, like the guppy, it eats the eggs of the mosquitoes carrying the malaria germ. Sparkling panchax are only suitable for a mixed aquarium because they become lazy when kept alone. They should be kept in an aquarium that has fish of the same size living farther down in the water. The sparkling panchax will eat any smaller fish living in its aquarium.

Aplocheilus lineatus comes from India and Ceylon. It grows up to 4 inches long and eats living and dried food.

Water temperature: 71.6° to 78.8°F.

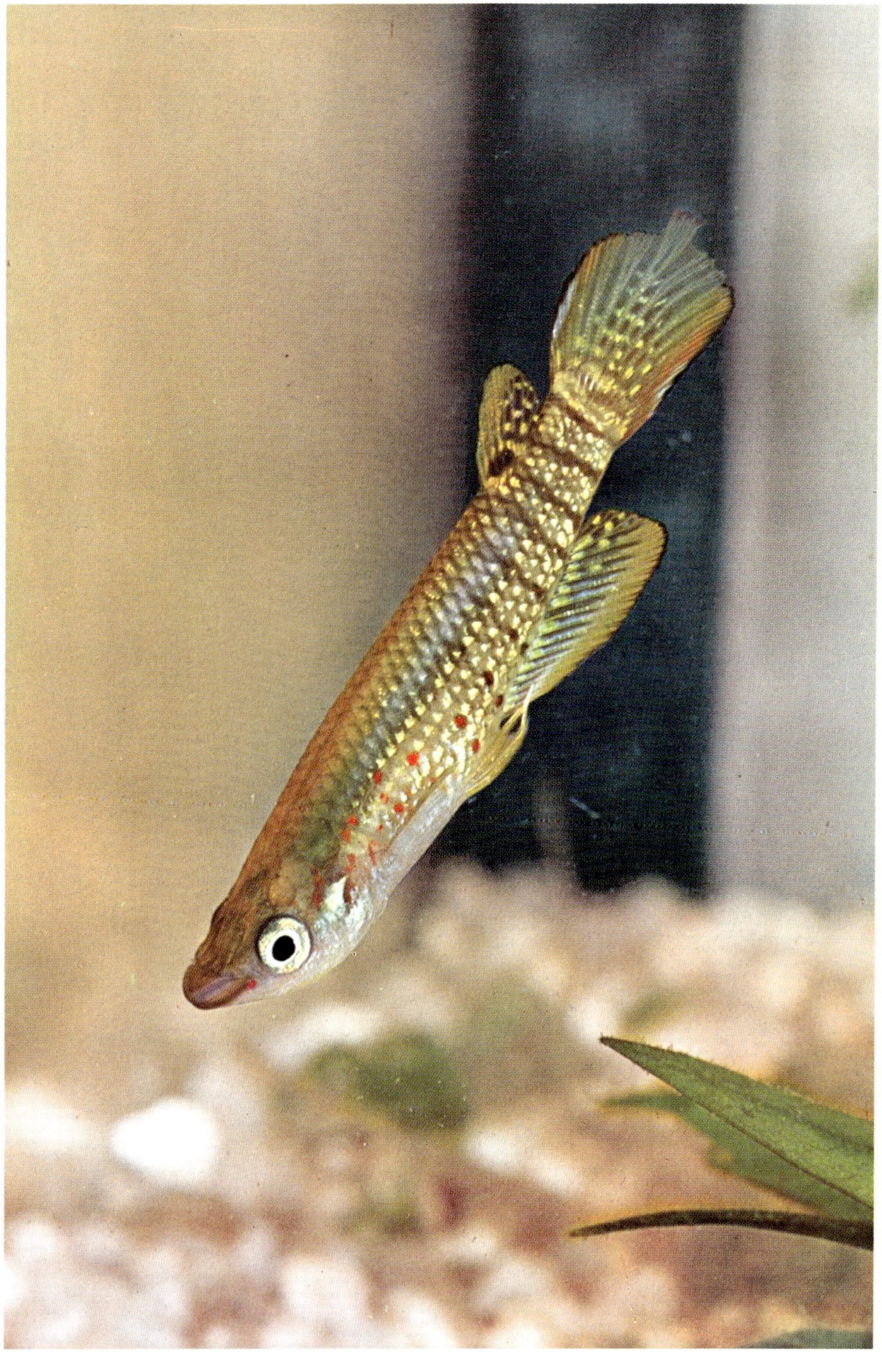

Zebra Danio

The zebra danio can be found living in large numbers in its natural environment of river, stream, or rice field. It is a suitable fish for the beginner to raise because it can be kept in an unheated room aquarium and can be bred easily. The males are slimmer and have brighter colors than the females. If you plan to breed zebra danio it is best to put plenty of pebbles on the bottom of a round glass bowl and fill it with water that has stood for a time. First place an egg-bearing female into the bowl. Two males can be placed in the bowl on another evening when fine weather can be expected the following day. Zebra danio prefer to mate when the sun is shining on them. When a male has enticed a female in among the plants, they press closely together and release eggs and sperm. As soon as this occurs the parent fish should be taken out, for they often will eat the eggs. When the young hatch they can be fed dried particles of food and small living food.

Danio (Brachydanio) rerio comes from India. It grows up to 2½ inches long and eats living and dried food.

Water temperature: 64.4° to 75.2°F.

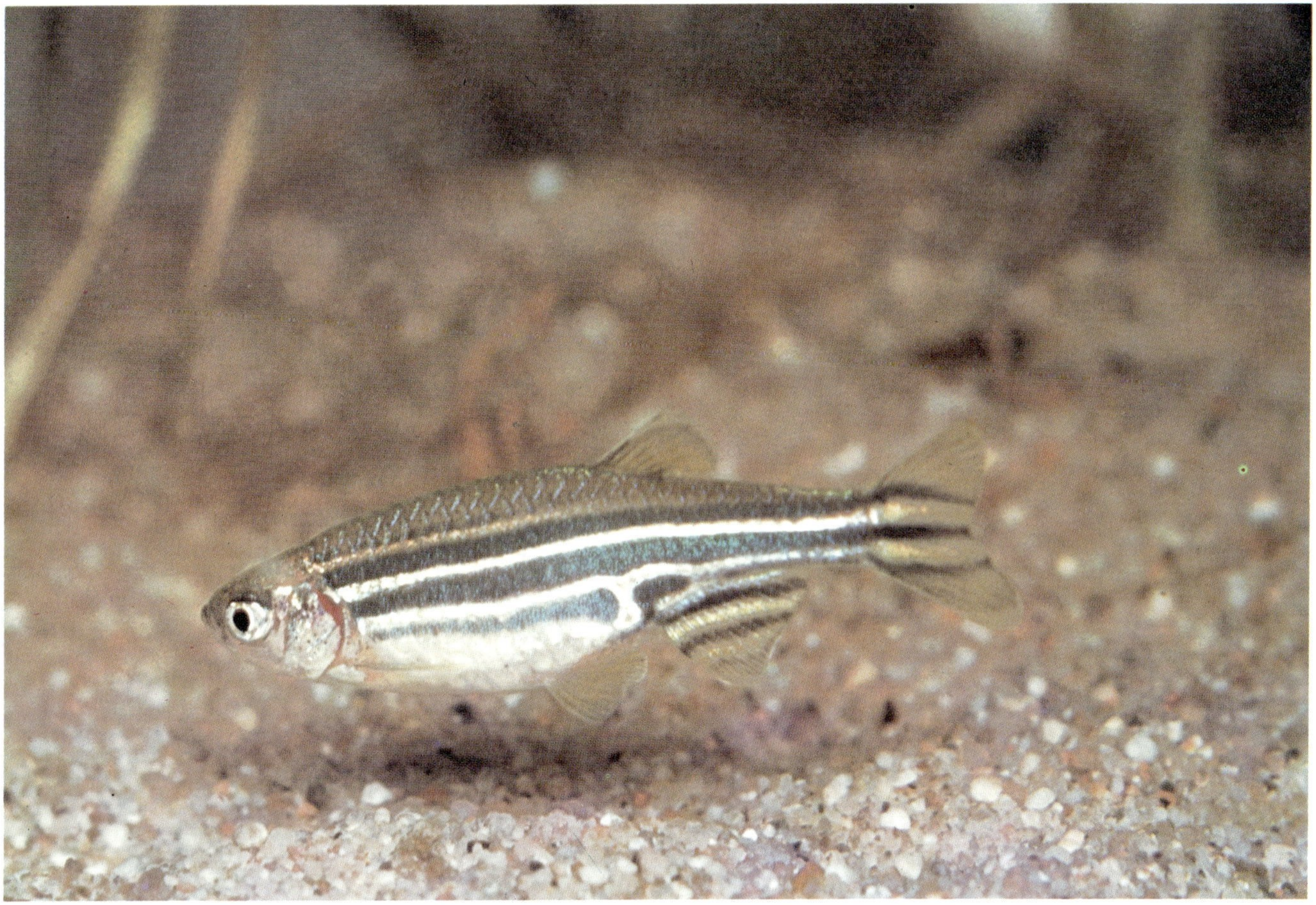

Pearl Danio

The pearl danio should be kept in large numbers in a long, well-planted aquarium with two males for every female. They are very lively fish and need plenty of swimming room. The coloring of the pearl danio is especially interesting, because it changes depending on the way the light falls on it. In sunlight the body of the pearl danio looks as green as grass, but in artificial lighting its colors vary from violet to blue. The blue-green edges of the cherry-red stripes on their sides can also appear to be lighter or darker depending on the light. Pearl danios prefer to live in sunny aquariums. Warm water is especially important during their breeding period, when they need a water temperature of 82.4°F.

Brachydanio albolineatus comes from Asia. It is 2 inches long and eats dried and living food.

Water temperature: 68° to 75.2°F.

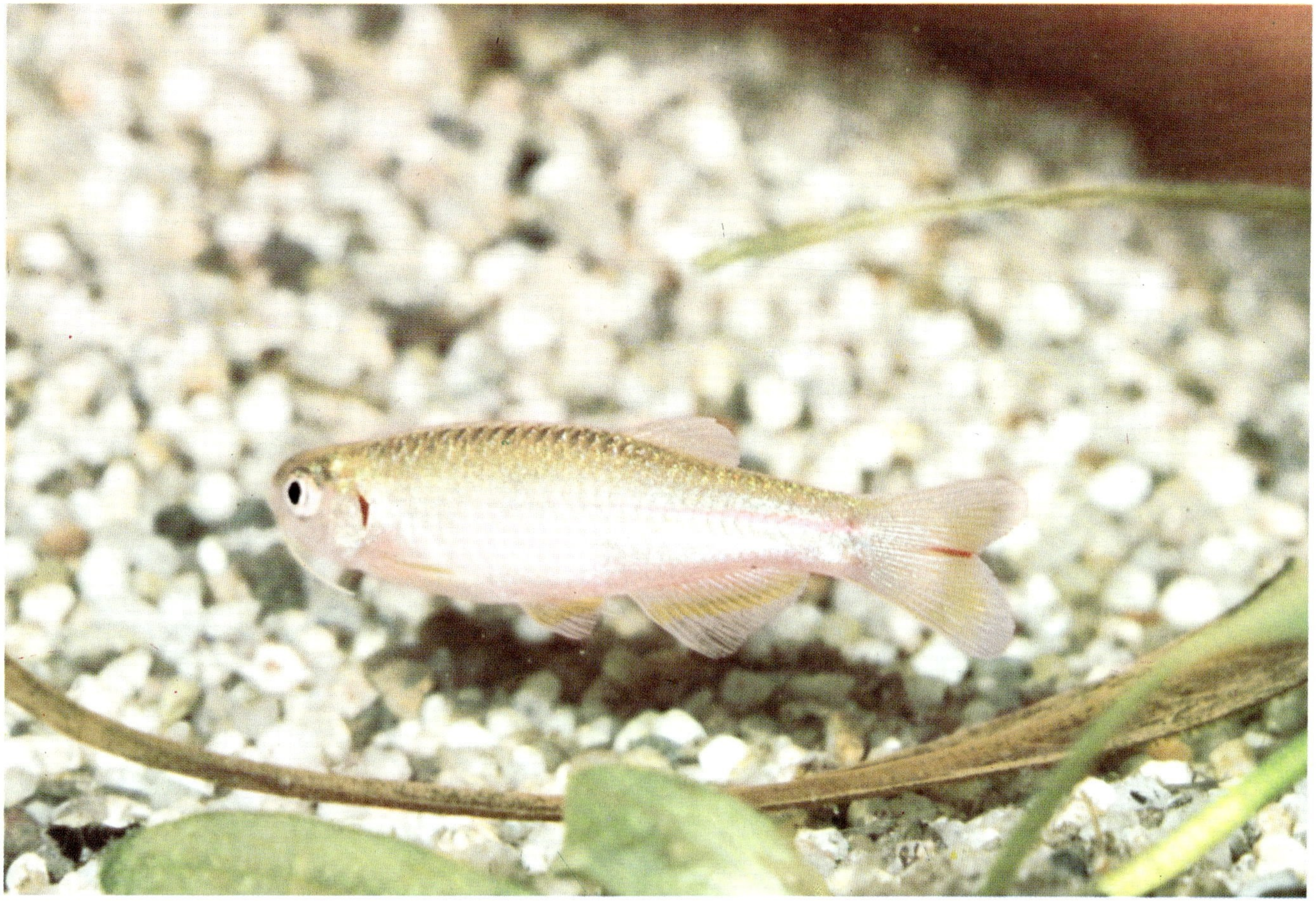

Sumatra or Tiger Barb

This distinctively marked fish is a very suitable occupant of a mixed aquarium. It must not, however, be kept with fish that have long fins because it will nibble at the fins and try to eat them. Because of this, angel fish, labyrinth fish, and glass catfish should not be kept with the sumatra barb. If only one sumatra barb is kept in an aquarium with other fish species it will become aggressive and begin to fight with them. It is best to keep a shoal of five to seven sumatra barbs together, for then they will choose one of the males in their group to be their leader, and will seldom trouble the other fish species in the aquarium. The coloring of the sumatra barb is shown off well in fluorescent lighting, and the contrast between the black stripes and the red fins is very attractive. These fish change colors according to their moods, but they assume their brightest colors during the breeding season. Occasionally sumatra barbs will turn upside down while swimming and look like they are standing on their heads in the water.

Barbus (Puntius) tetrazona comes from Sumatra. It grows up to 2 inches long and eats living and dried food.

Water temperature: 68° to 78.8°F.

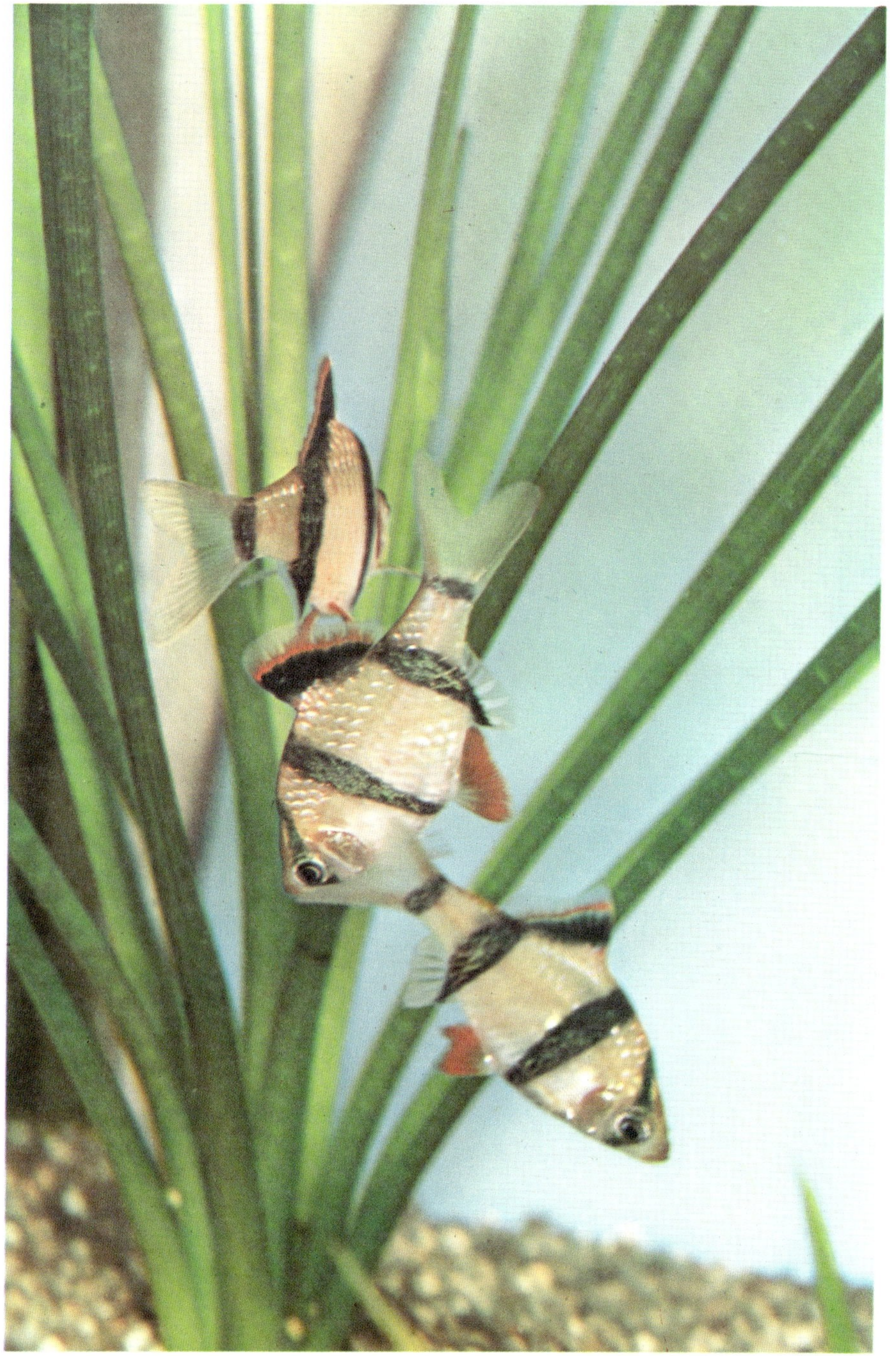

Golden Barb

The scientific classification for the golden barb has not yet been established. Its origin is uncertain; when it was discovered in America, it was thought to be a hybrid, or specially bred variety of another fish. The older the golden barb becomes, the more its golden coloring shines. When it feels well, its fins become a deeper red. Like other fish we have mentioned, golden barbs should never be kept individually. It is necessary to have at least two of these fish together for them to live peacefully. They can be easily kept in a mixed aquarium. Fresh water should be added to their aquarium regularly because they are sensitive to water which is too old. Fresh water also increases their willingness to breed.

Barbus (Puntius) schuberti is 3 inches long. It eats dried and living food.

Water temperature: 71.6° to 75.2°F.

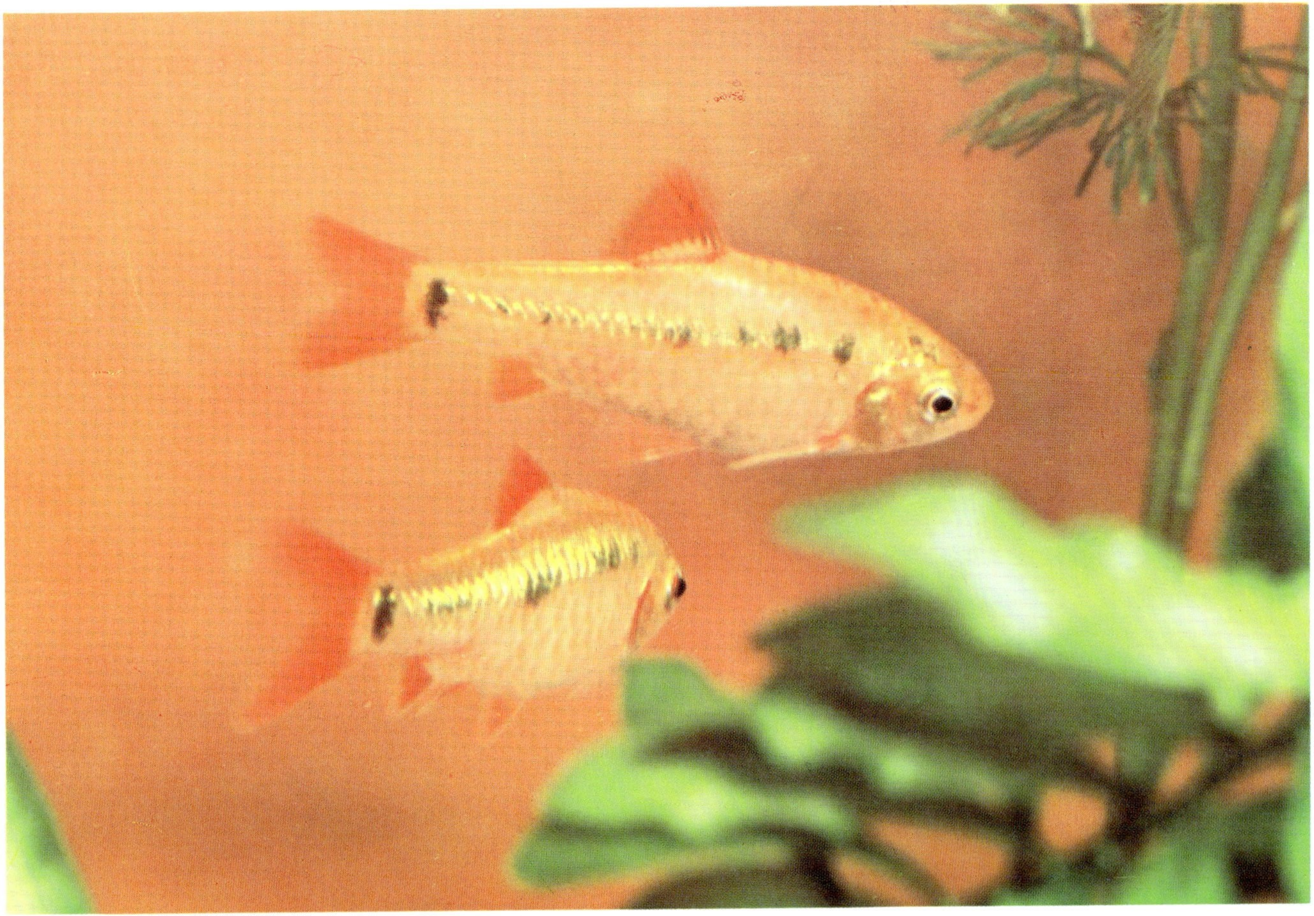

Rosy Barb

The rosy barb is one of the most beautiful of the tropical fish suitable for an unheated room aquarium. Its natural setting is northern India, Bengal, and Assam, where it is found in large numbers. It may grow to a length of 6 inches, but does not grow as large in the aquarium. When it is 3 inches long it is sexually mature, and then the males show their beautiful colors. The back of the rosy barb is a moss green color and the sides look as if red ink had been spilled over them. The dorsal fin is jet black. Our picture shows that these fish are an attractive addition to an aquarium even before they display their mating colors. The rosy barb is very lively. It can often be seen eagerly searching for food among the rotting plants on the bottom of the aquarium. If the water is too cold, these fish will become lazy and will show very little color. Their water should be warm for breeding.

Barbus (Puntius) conchonius grows up to 6 inches long and eats both living and dried food.

Water temperature: 53.6° to 75.2°F.

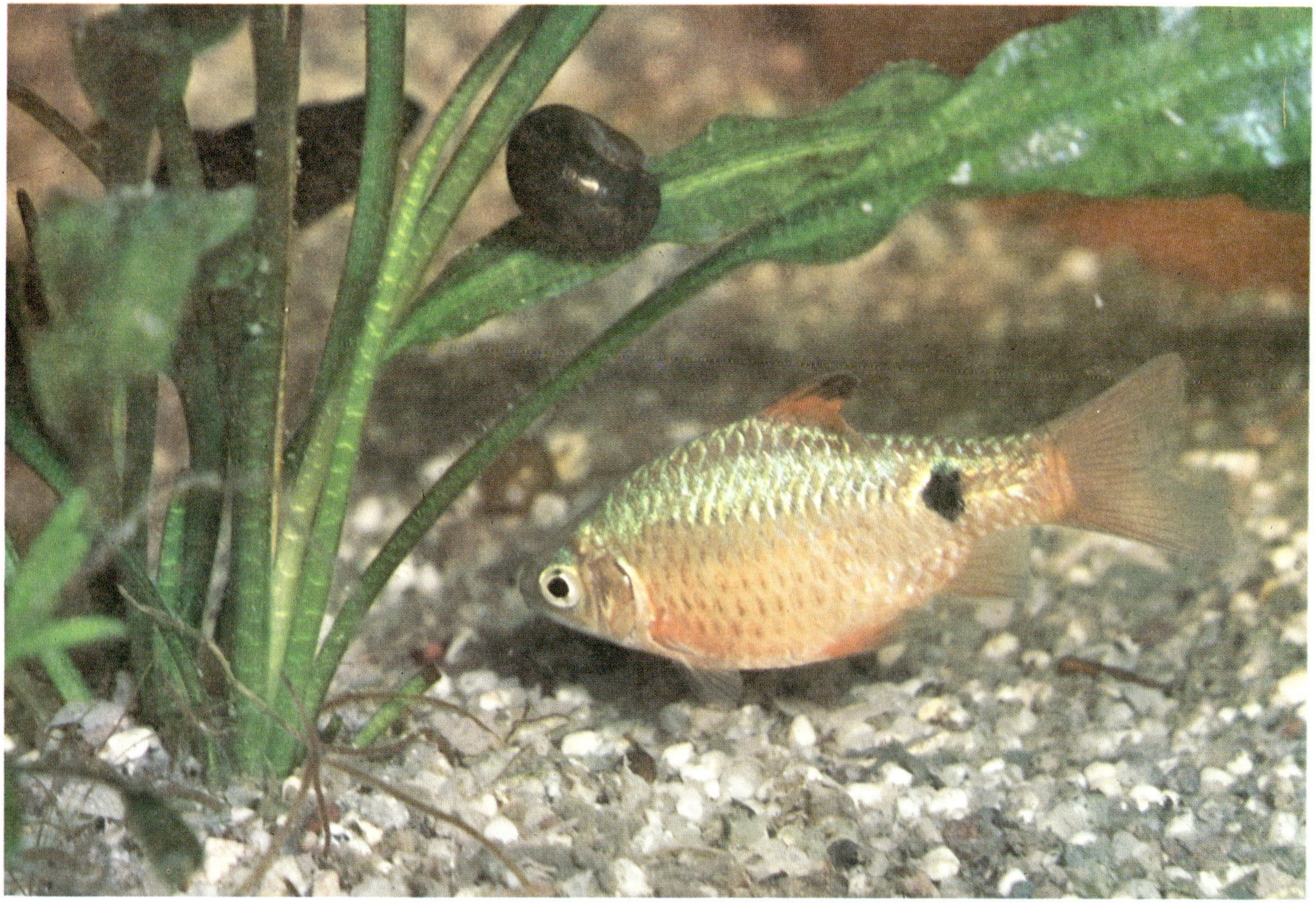

Harlequin Fish

This fish should be kept in shallow water that has abundant plant life. The water in the fish's natural setting is extremely soft and its temperature often rises quite high during the day. Because harlequin fish do not make contact with other fish very easily, several should be kept together. Breeding the harlequin fish is rather difficult, but fish imports are now being shipped by plane and successful breeding is more possible now than it was in past years. If two fish in a shoal seem to get on well together, a glass bowl should be prepared for breeding. The bottom of the bowl should be covered with soaked strands of peat and a cryptocoryne plant should be placed in the middle. The water should be soft and have a temperature of over 78.8°F. The fish will then spawn pressed closely together on the undersides of leaves.

Rasbora heteromorpha comes from Thailand, Malaya, and Sumatra. It grows up to 2 inches long and eats dried and living foods.

Water temperature: 71.6° to 78.8°F.

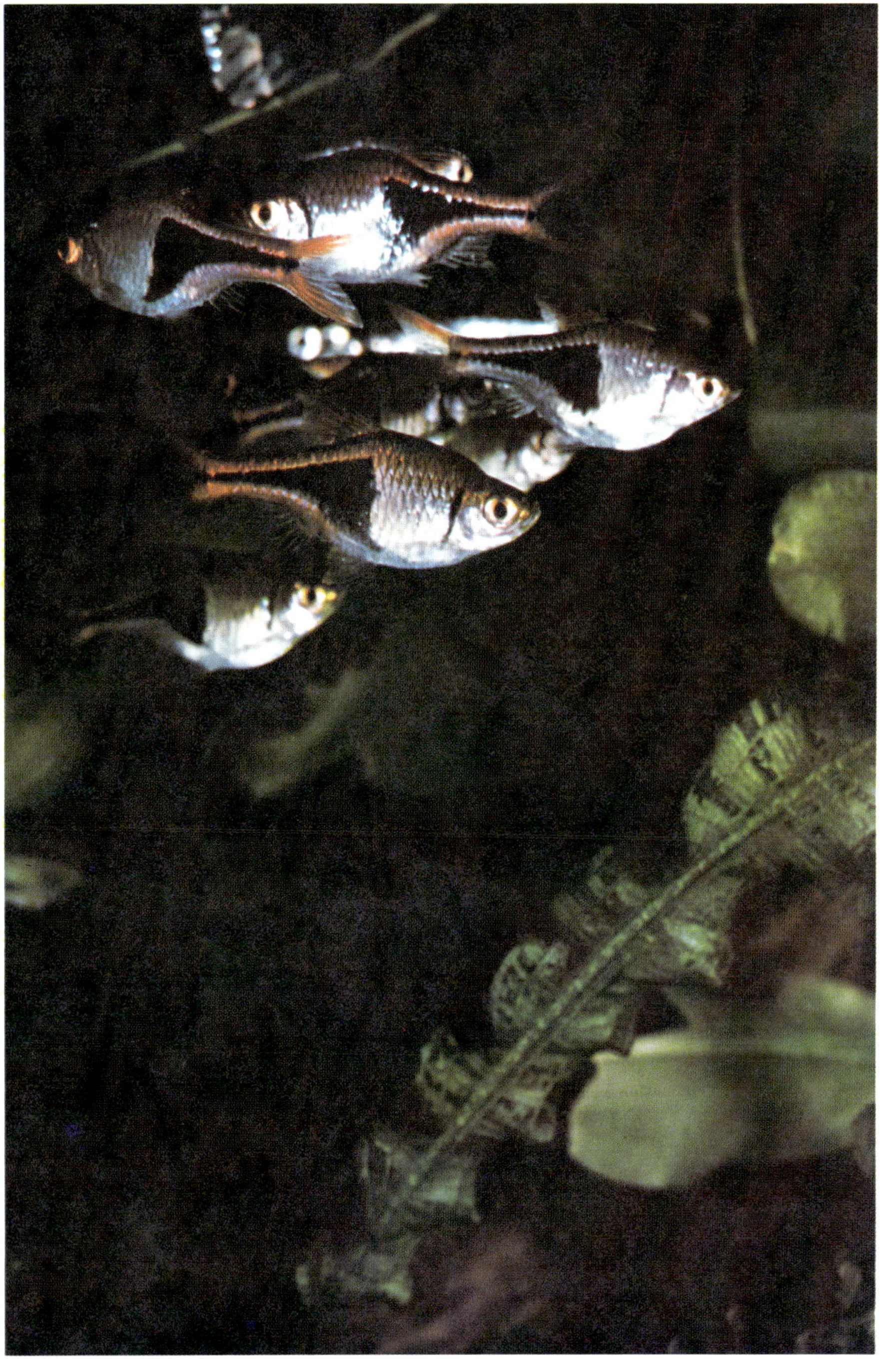

Sucking Gyrinocheilus

In 1955 the sucking gyrinocheilus was imported from Thailand (formerly Siam) where it lives in large numbers in quickly flowing streams. It is happy in any kind of water. As a young fish it can live on the bottom of the aquarium with practically every other kind of fish. It sucks along the aquarium glass and plants and eats all the algae without causing any of the damage to the aquarium plants that snails often do. When it is older it becomes less easy going and sometimes will chase other fish. The fish is also interesting from a biological point of view: most fish suck in air through the mouth and expel it through the gills, but the sucking gyrinocheilus has a second opening above the usual gill where it takes in air. It therefore can use its mouth exclusively for eating.

Gyrinocheilus aymonieri grows up to 10 inches long and eats algae.

Water temperature: approximately 77°F.

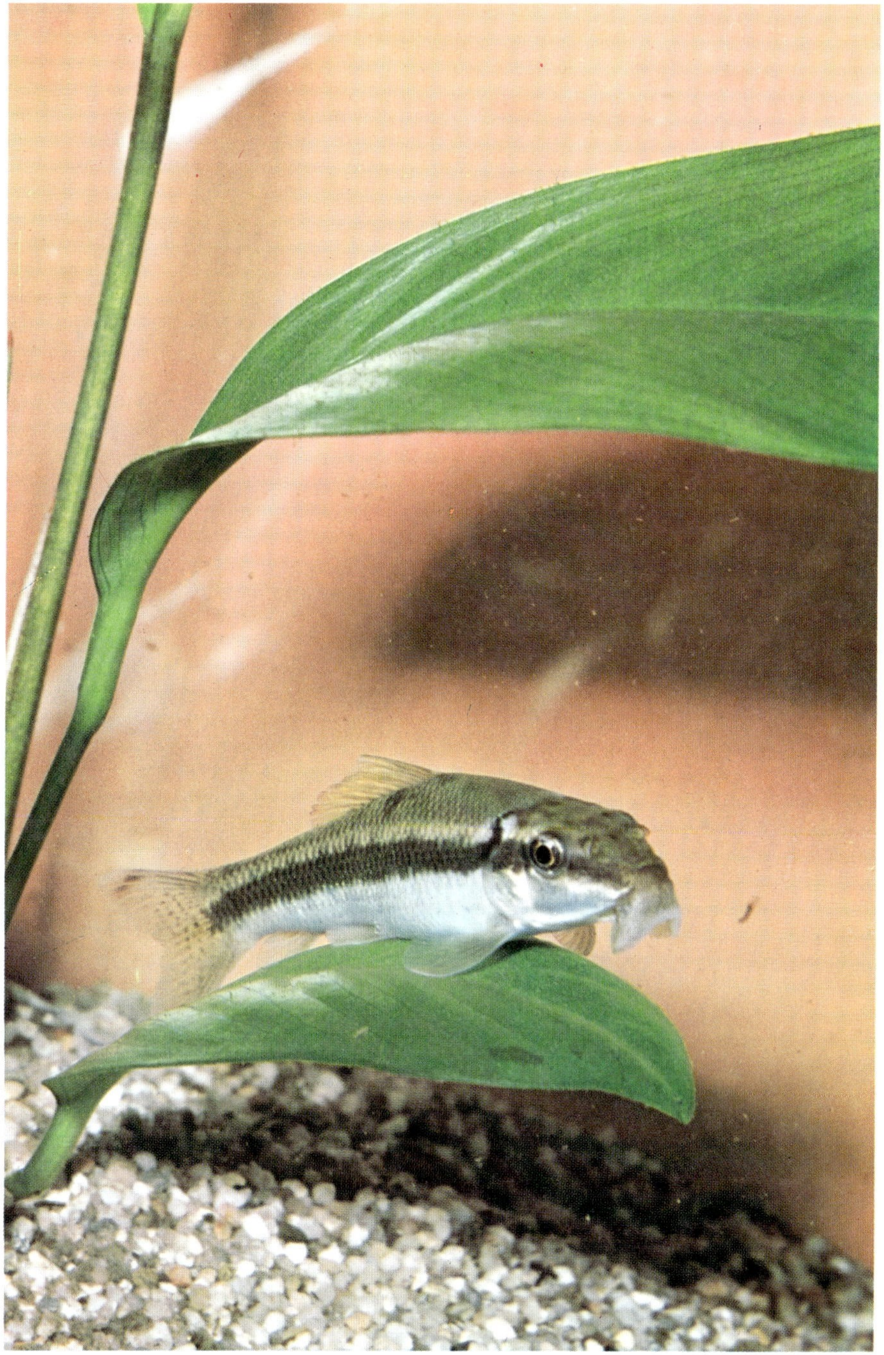

Clown Loach

The clown loach is another fish that should be kept in a group. If a clown loach is the only one of its kind in an aquarium it will either remain shy or become aggressive towards other fish. It loves hiding places, and these can easily be provided by using flat pieces of coconut shell or stones. A clown loach will lie in wait behind these objects until it sees some food. These fish also need swimming room because they like to swim around in a shoal. If their leader settles on one stone, the whole group will follow him. The vertical orange and black stripes on the clown loach's body are very colorful. Clown loaches seem to be attracted to fish with similar coloring. They will often join the orange-and-black-striped sumatra barbs in the aquarium even though these fish have a completely different body shape.

Botia macracantha comes from Indonesia. It grows up to 6 inches long and eats plants, and dried and living foods.

Water temperature: 68° to 77°F.

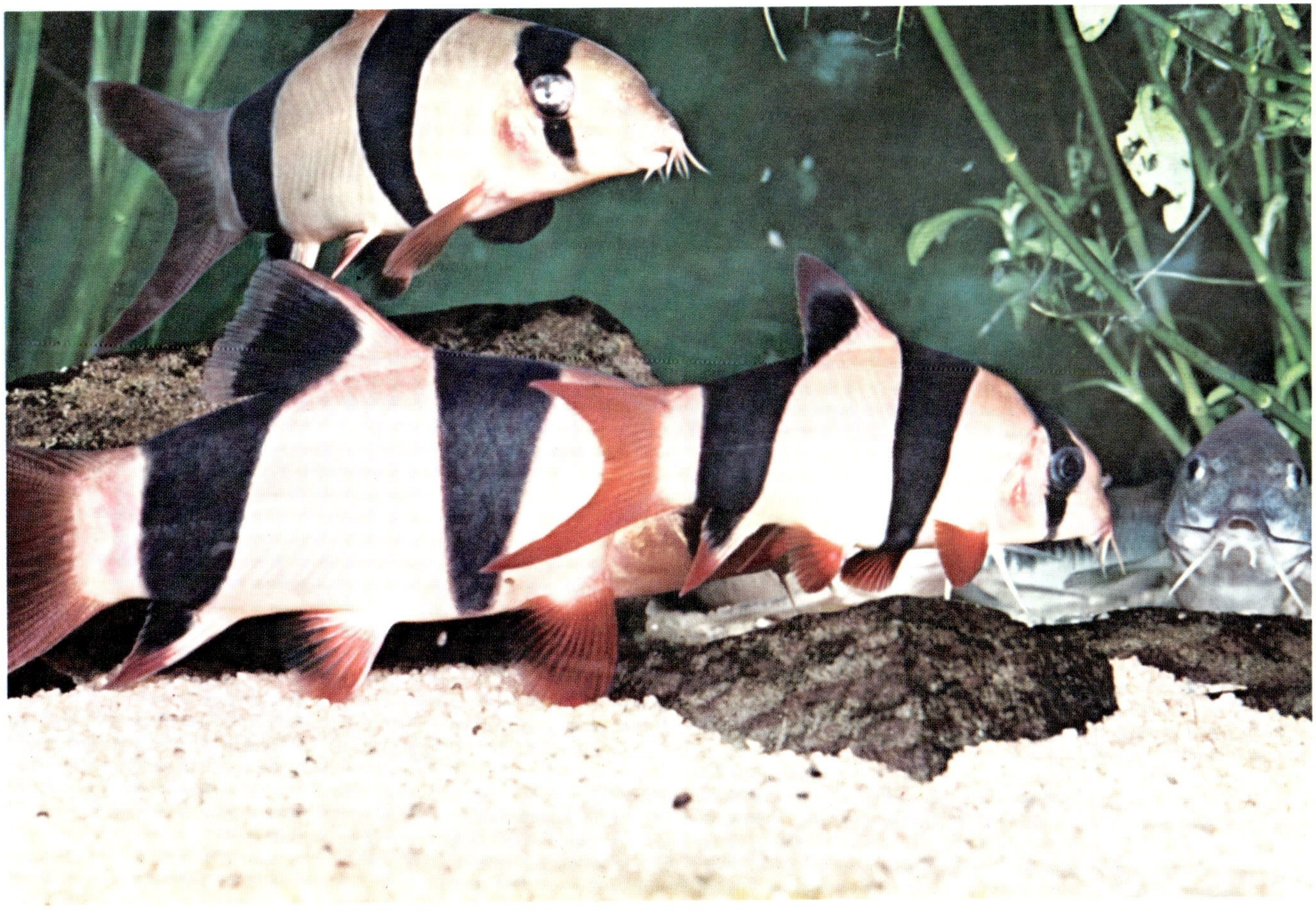

Red-tailed Black Shark

The coloring of this fish is an unusual and striking combination of red and black. The wild variety of red-tailed black shark lives in small, well-planted streams. In the aquarium it prefers soft peaty water and likes to hide in hollow stones or tree roots. This does not keep it from being seen, however. It is quite an active fish, and can almost always be seen as it takes up its position and darts out to catch food, pick up algae, or scare off another fish. Unfortunately, older black sharks are very aggressive. For this reason it is best to buy very small fish of this species. These are more difficult to keep than the larger sizes, but the smaller fish do not fight and have marvelously large fins for their body size. It is possible to tell right away whether or not a black shark feels happy. If it is in bad spirits it is a brownish color with an orange tail fin. If it feels happy, its deep red tail fin will shine out against the jet black body.

Labeo bicolor comes from Thailand. It grows up to 6 inches long and eats dried food, worms, and algae.

Water temperature: 68° to 75.2°F.

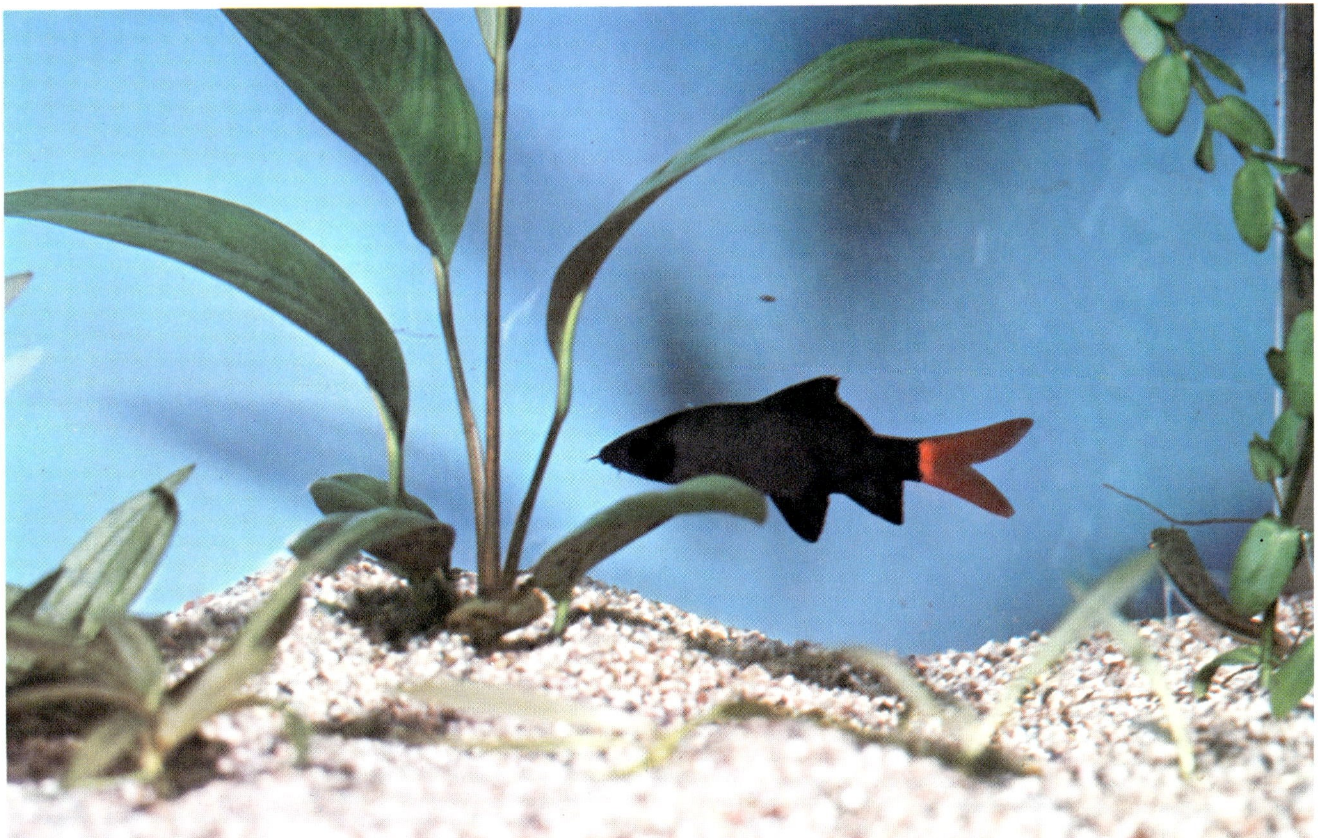

Bronze Corydoras or Catfish

The shape of this catfish makes it well suited to life on the bottom of an aquarium. Its belly is flat and its mouth is positioned low on its body. Barbels (small feeler-like projections) are attached to its mouth, and these aid the fish as it grovels along the bottom in search of food. The bronze corydoras has armor on both sides which consists of rows of bone plating arranged like tiles. This does not hinder its movement, for these fish can move easily. When they are young they like to swim in the middle water levels. They are an easy fish to keep in an aquarium because they can live in any temperature or hardness of water. They have an additional breathing apparatus similar to that of other catfish and the gyrinocheilus. The fish swallows air, the oxygen is taken into the blood in the large intestine, and the used air is expelled through a back passage. This is why the catfish is able to live in even the worst water conditions.

Corydoras aeneus comes from South America. It grows up to 2 inches long and eats rotting plants and living food.

Water temperature: 64.4° to 77°F.

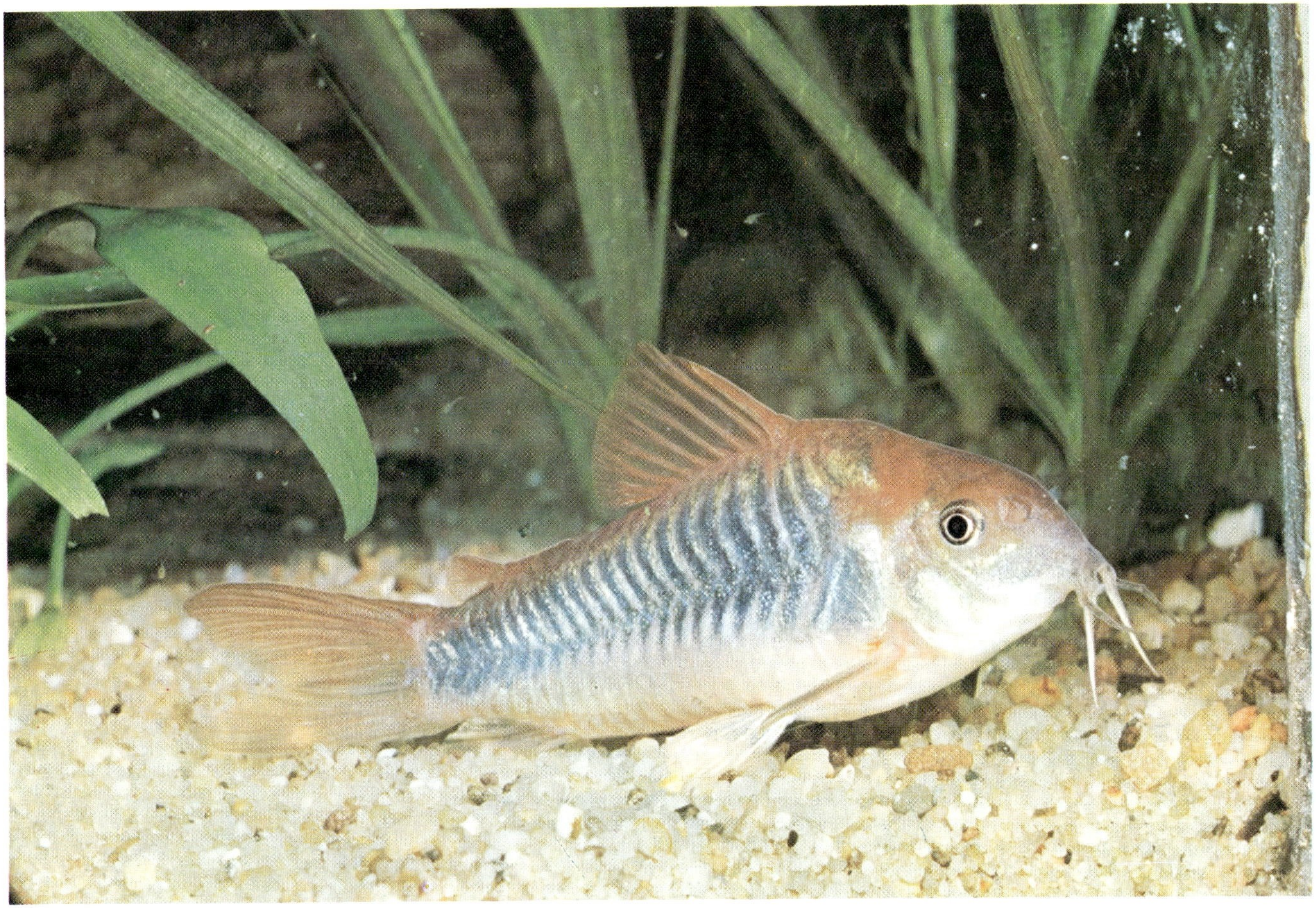

Glass Catfish or Ghost Fish

The only way to study the anatomy of a fish without cutting it open is to find and observe a transparent fish. There are completely transparent varieties in most fish species; glass fish, glass rasboras, glass catfish, glass barbs, and glass tetras are a few of these. The glass catfish is striking not only because it is transparent but also because its yellow body is able to shine in all the colors of the rainbow when light falls on it. In our picture its coloring looks blue, but if the camera had been held a little lower in the same light, the fish would have looked quite a different color. It has two very long barbels on the upper jaw, and the careful observer will notice that the dorsal fin consists of a single ray. Glass catfish should be kept in shoals in a well-planted aquarium. They swim in the daytime and rest at night.

Kryptopterus bicirrhis comes from Thailand and Indonesia. It grows up to 4 inches long and eats living foods.

Water temperature: 71.6° to 82.4°F.

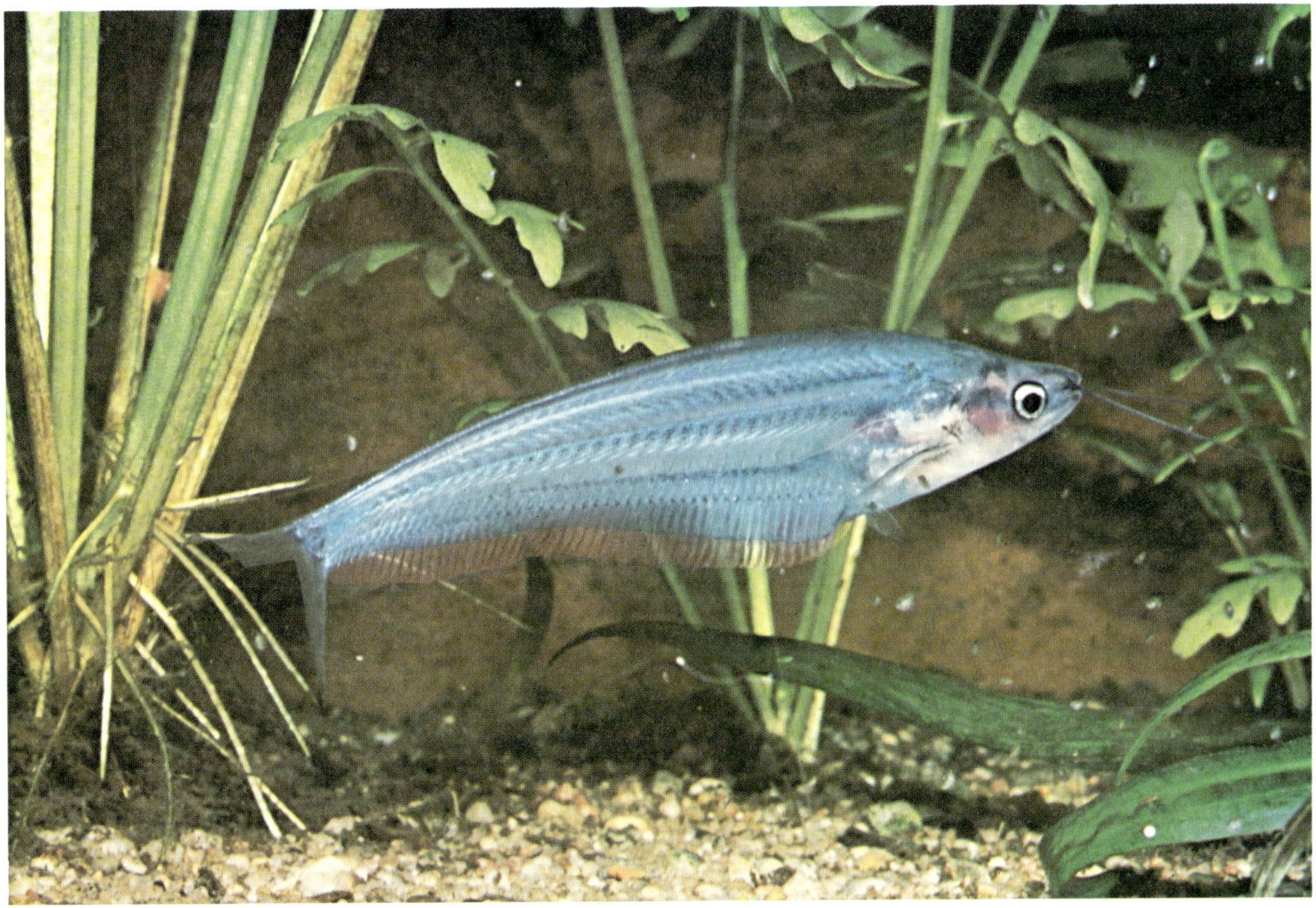

Indian Glass Fish

By observing their behavior one can tell that young glass fish are used to a lazy life. They do not chase their food. They only eat whatever comes directly in front of their mouths. The aquarist who has successfully bred a couple of glass fish must make sure that their offspring have food dangled in front of them. Otherwise the young fish could die of hunger in the middle of a good hunting ground from sheer inborn laziness. Adult glass fish are much easier to keep than the young glass fish. When these fish are newly introduced to an aquarium they are quite often shy. They will soon become confident, however, if other quiet fish species are put in with them. They also feel much more at home if approximately five teaspoons of salt are added to their water. Glass fish are particularly beautiful during their mating period when the edges of the male's fins turn a bright blue.

Chanda ranga comes from India and Burma. It grows up to 2 inches long and eats living food.

Water temperature: 69.8° to 77°F.

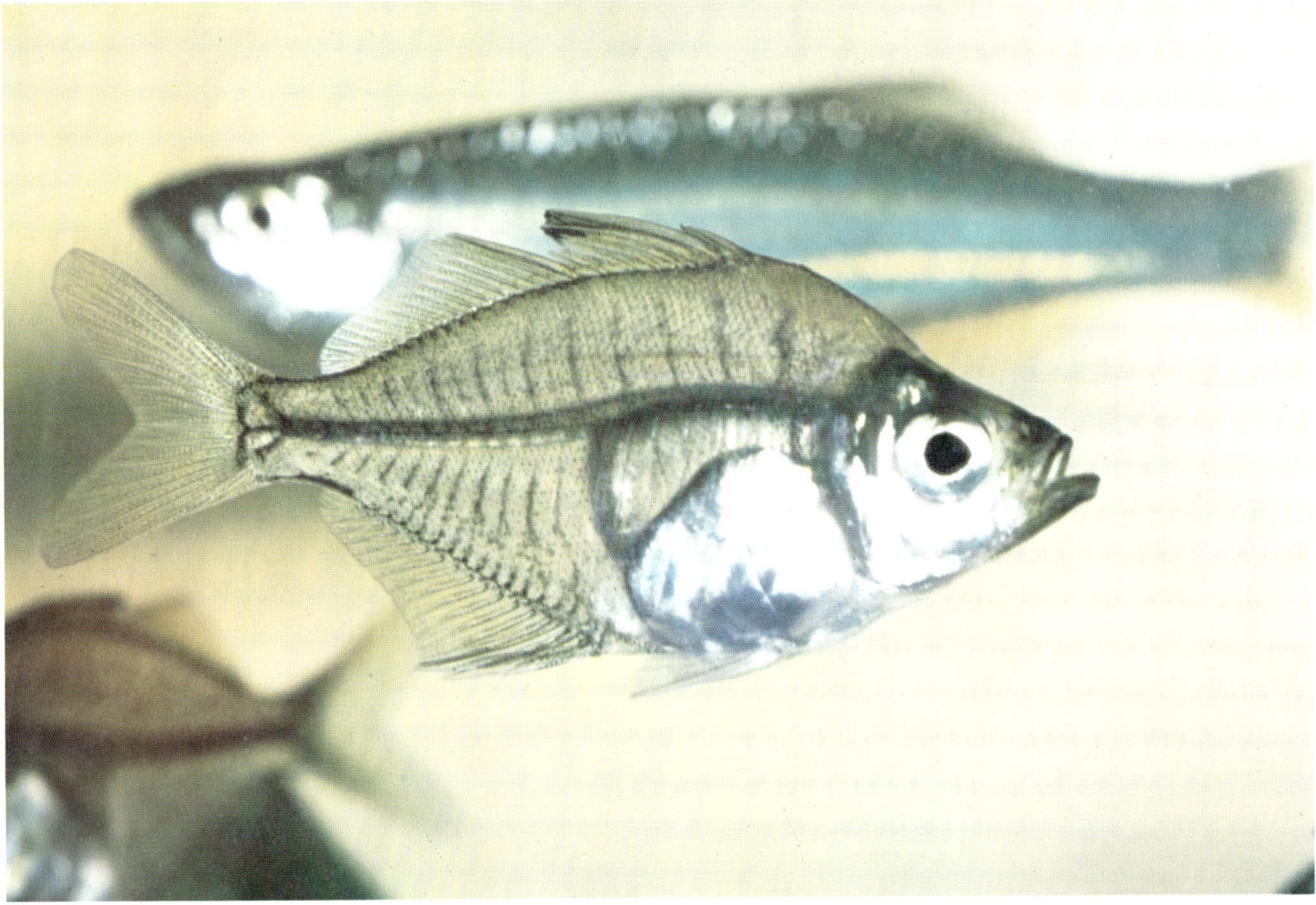

Pumpkinseed

Before it reaches maturity the pumpkinseed can easily be kept in a well-planted aquarium, but it is often too big to live in an aquarium when fully grown. During the last few years aquarists have placed the large adult pumpkinseeds in rivers and lakes. In the winter the pumpkinseed needs water temperatures of around 41°F. The colors of both the male and the female are brighter in the summer, but during the mating period the female develops the brightest colors. The female lays her eggs in a hollow and the male guards the eggs and fans fresh water over them with his breast fin. The young hatch after three to five days and at first remain in the nest. At this time the male remains by the nest and guards it so loyally that he can even be caught by hand. Unlike some fish, the pumpkinseed parents do not continue to guard their young or lead them around after they hatch. When the young are a few days old they leave the nest and cling to plants. Pumpkinseeds do not receive their brightest colors until they are three years old.

Lepomis gibbosus comes from the United States. It grows up to 7 inches long.

Water temperature: 41° to 71.6°F.

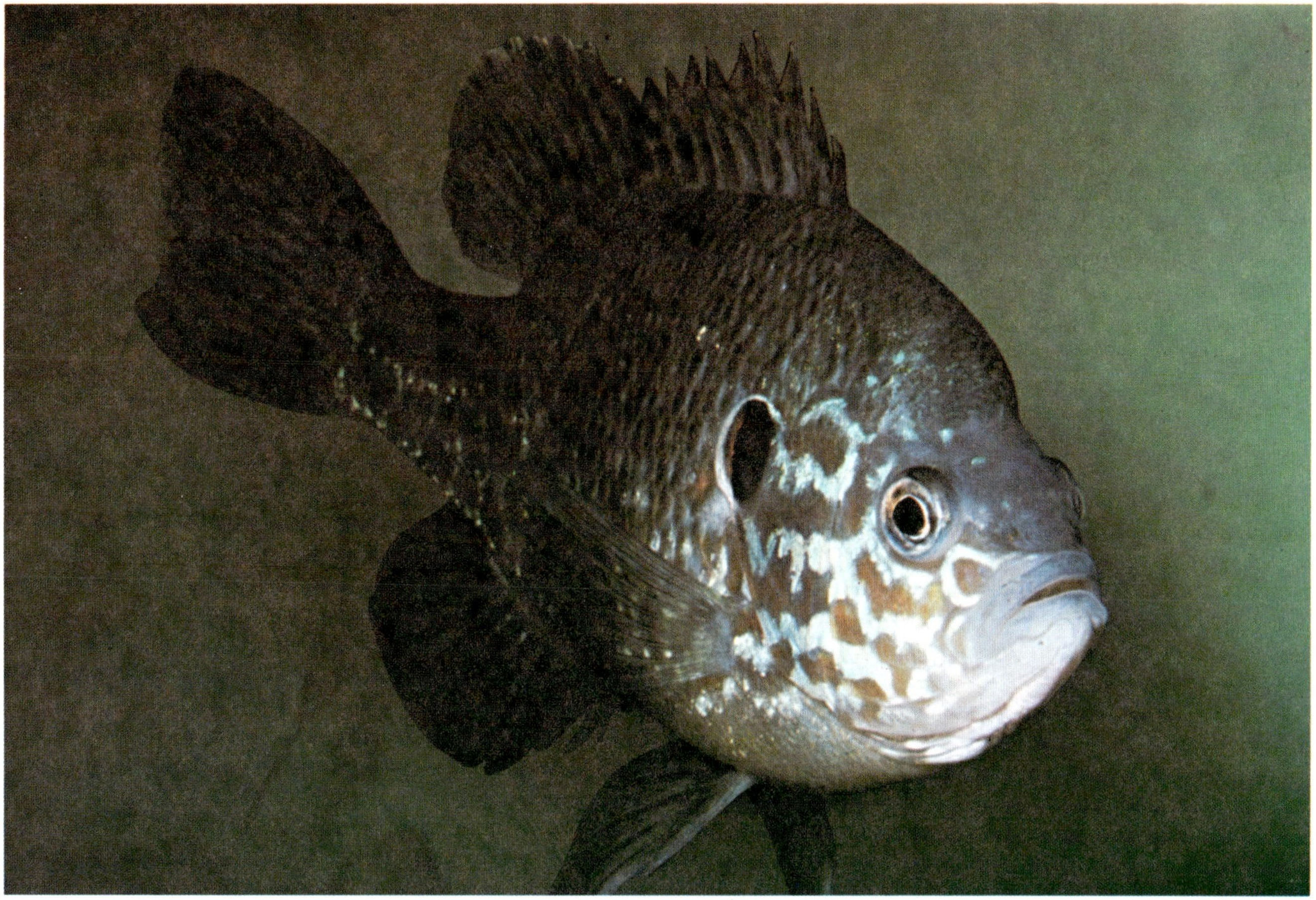

Ramirezi's Dwarf Cichlid

Of all the cichlid varieties, this fish is the most beautiful. Both the male and female fish are so colorful that they can hardly be distinguished from each other. Research has been done on the behavior of the cichlids, and it has been found that they care for their young very diligently. It has also been discovered that the dwarf cichlid has a varied emotional life, and its coloring changes in relation to its changes in emotion. The person who prefers a well-planted small aquarium for his studies would do well to obtain this small fish. Unlike the large cichlids, the dwarf cichlids seldom dig up the ground of the aquarium and do not bite off plants. They are also easy to care for because they are a small fish and can be kept in mixed aquariums in soft water. The only disadvantages in raising the dwarf cichlid seem to be that it has a tendency to become ill and has a short life span of about two years.

Apistogramma ramirezi comes from Venezuelan tributaries of the Orinoco River. It grows to be 2 inches long and eats small living food.

Water temperature: 71.6° to 86°F.

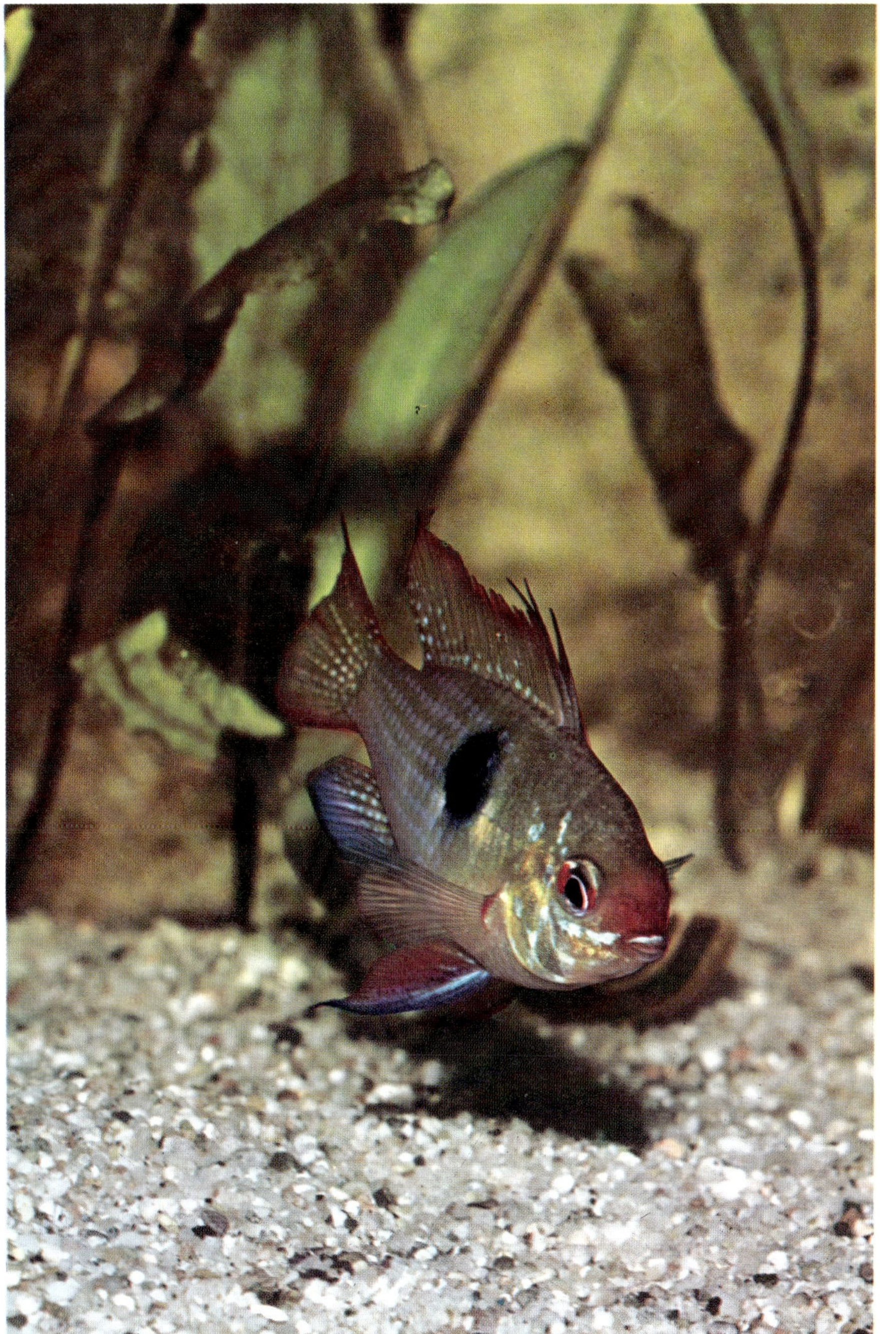

Peacock or Dwarf Rainbow Cichlid

In most fish species the male is much more colorful than the female, but this is reversed in the peacock cichlid. The females are more colorful than the males and can be recognized by a much deeper red mark on the side. The courtship and mating habits of the peacock cichlid are very rough. The couple grab hold of each other by the mouth and twist and drag each other around the aquarium, often bending their bodies into an S-shape or pressing close together. The female lays the fertilized eggs in hollows. When the young hatch they are taken care of by both parents, but the female takes a more active part in their care. The young fish are led by their parents for a long time. Like the dwarf cichlids, the colors of the peacock cichlids change with their emotions, and the young fish react very strongly to their parents' change of color. At the first sign of displeasure or danger the young fish sink motionless to the bottom and will not swim again until their parents give them a new sign.

Pelmatochromis kribensis comes from tropical West Africa. It grows to 3 or 4 inches long and eats living food.

Water temperature: **78.8° to 86°F.**

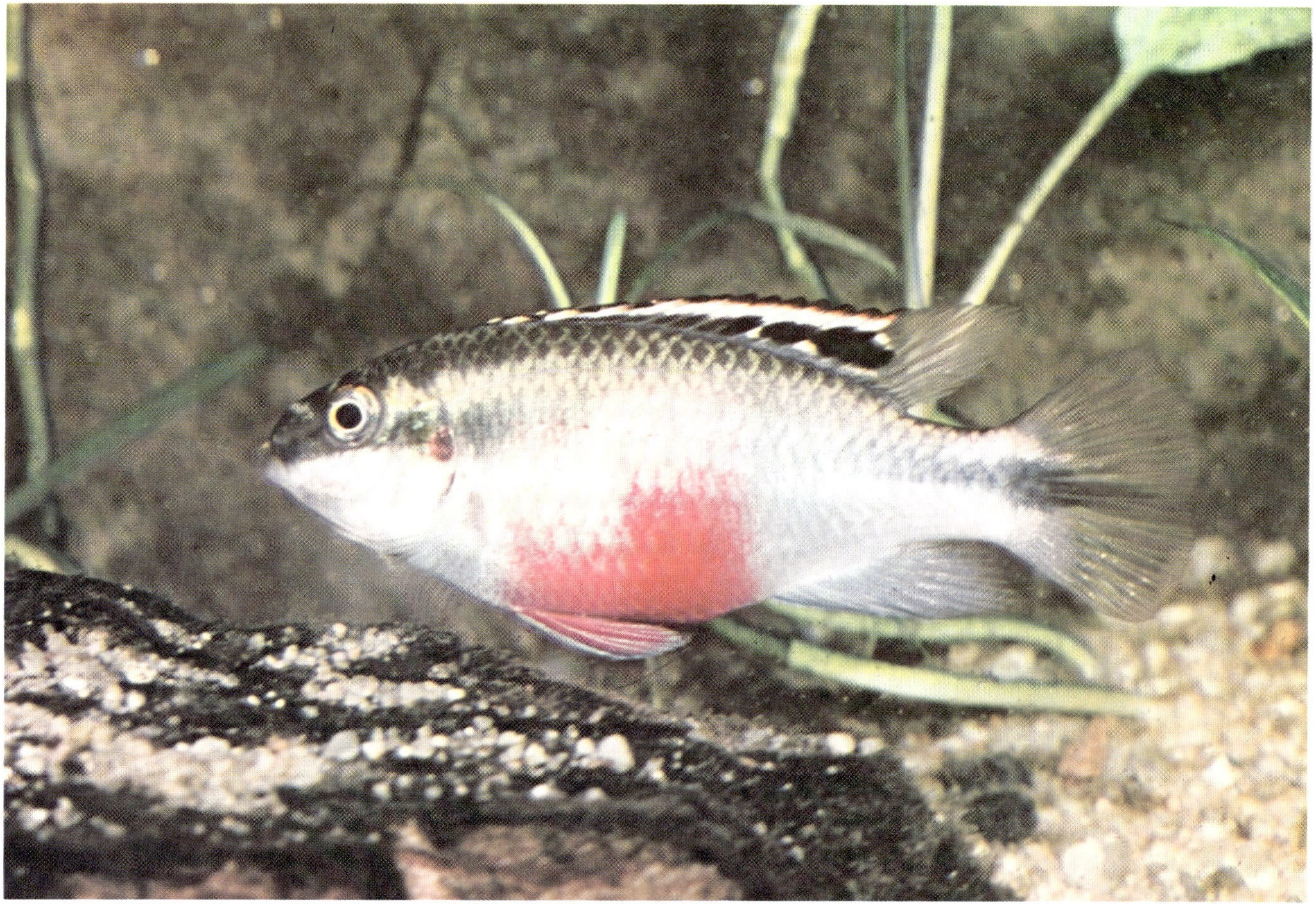

Blue or Texas Cichlid

This high-backed cichlid can be found mainly in the waters of the Rio Grande in Mexico and rivers in Texas. It is a favorite food of people in these areas and is caught with fishing rods or in wicker traps. In its natural environment it can grow up to 10 or 12 inches long, but it remains smaller in the aquarium. When they are 3 or 4 inches long the couples begin mating. They prepare their nest by upsetting the bottom of the aquarium and scooping out large mouthfuls of sand to form a hollow. They uproot any plants still remaining upright. The eggs are laid into the hollow and guarded by both parents who continually fan fresh water over them with their breast fins. During this period the coloring of the parents changes from blue and mother-of-pearl spots on a dark background to a cream color. The belly and chest part of the female become jet black. Unfortunately, the blue cichlid is very aggressive and may eat its own young.

Herichthys cyanoguttatus grows up to 10 or 12 inches long and eats living food.

Water temperature: 60.8° to 82.4°F.

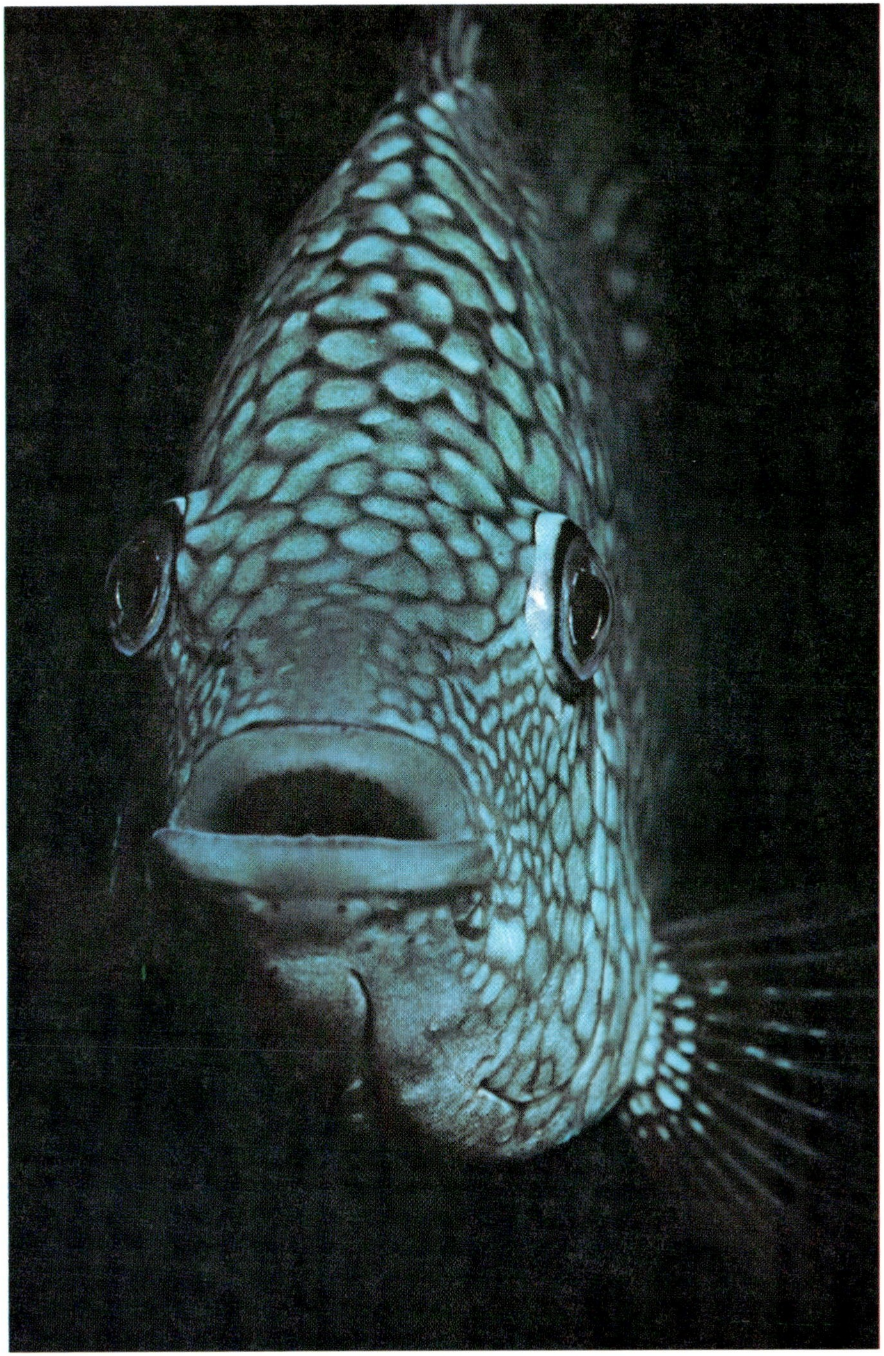

Mother-of-Pearl Cichlid

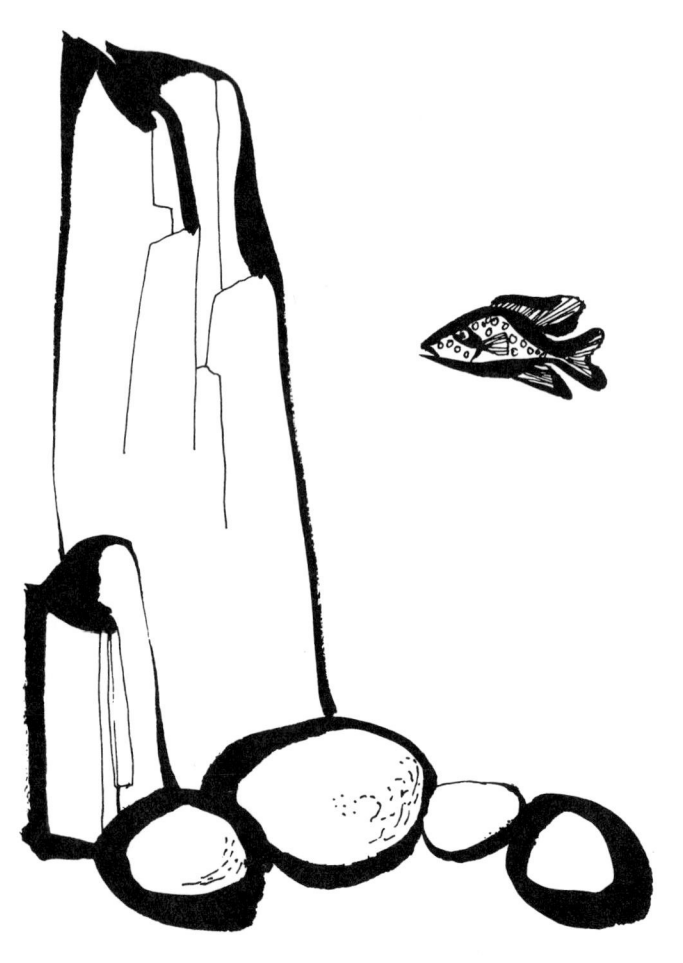

This fish is usually not suitable for the aquarium. It turns up the ground of its aquarium more than any other cichlid, and during mating time it makes large spawning holes in the bottom of the aquarium and carries large amounts of sand around in its mouth. It lays its eggs in a hollow and carefully watches them. When the young fish hatch they are led around for a long time in a group. The parents take more care of their brood if they have to defend them against other fish in the aquarium. If every distraction is kept away, the fighting spirit of the adult fish takes another turn and instead of chasing away intruders, the parent fish chase and eat their own young. These bad qualities will disappear if there are many adult fish in a small aquarium and many places at the back of the aquarium where the young fish can hide.

Geophagus acuticeps comes from the Amazon River region. It grows up to 10 inches long and eats living food.

Water temperature: 71.6° to 82.4°F.

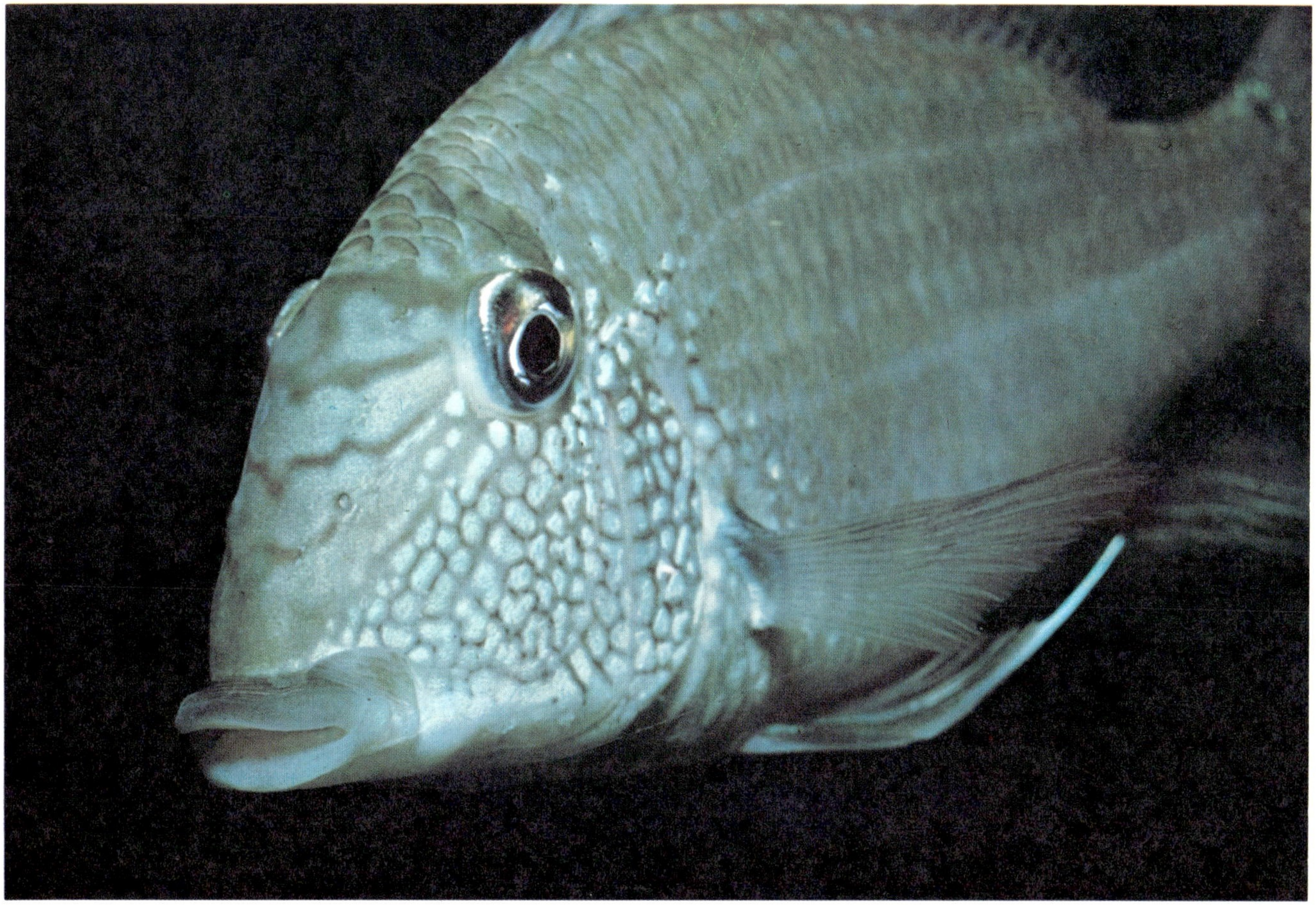

Banded Cichlid

The banded cichlid is a distinctive fish only because it has shining red eyes and a black line joining two eye-shaped spots on the dorsal and anal (bottom) fins. Like all cichlids, it is aggressive towards other fish and tends to alter life in the aquarium to suit itself. Many sensitive plants quickly die when damaged or uprooted by the banded cichlid. Large pools of water decorated with stones or tree roots are the best habitat for the banded cichlid. Robust plants whose roots are protected by heavy stones can also be used in its aquarium. Experiments have found that large cichlids lose their unpleasant qualities if they have enough room in their living areas. The individual fish form their own territories and will threaten their opponents on the invisible territory borders. They will never seriously attack them, however, if their own areas are large enough. The banded cichlid also needs to have a large living area if it is to fully develop the habits and gestures characteristic of its species.

Cichlasoma severum comes from South America. It grows to 8 inches long and eats living food of all kinds.

Water temperature: 73.4° to 82.4°F.

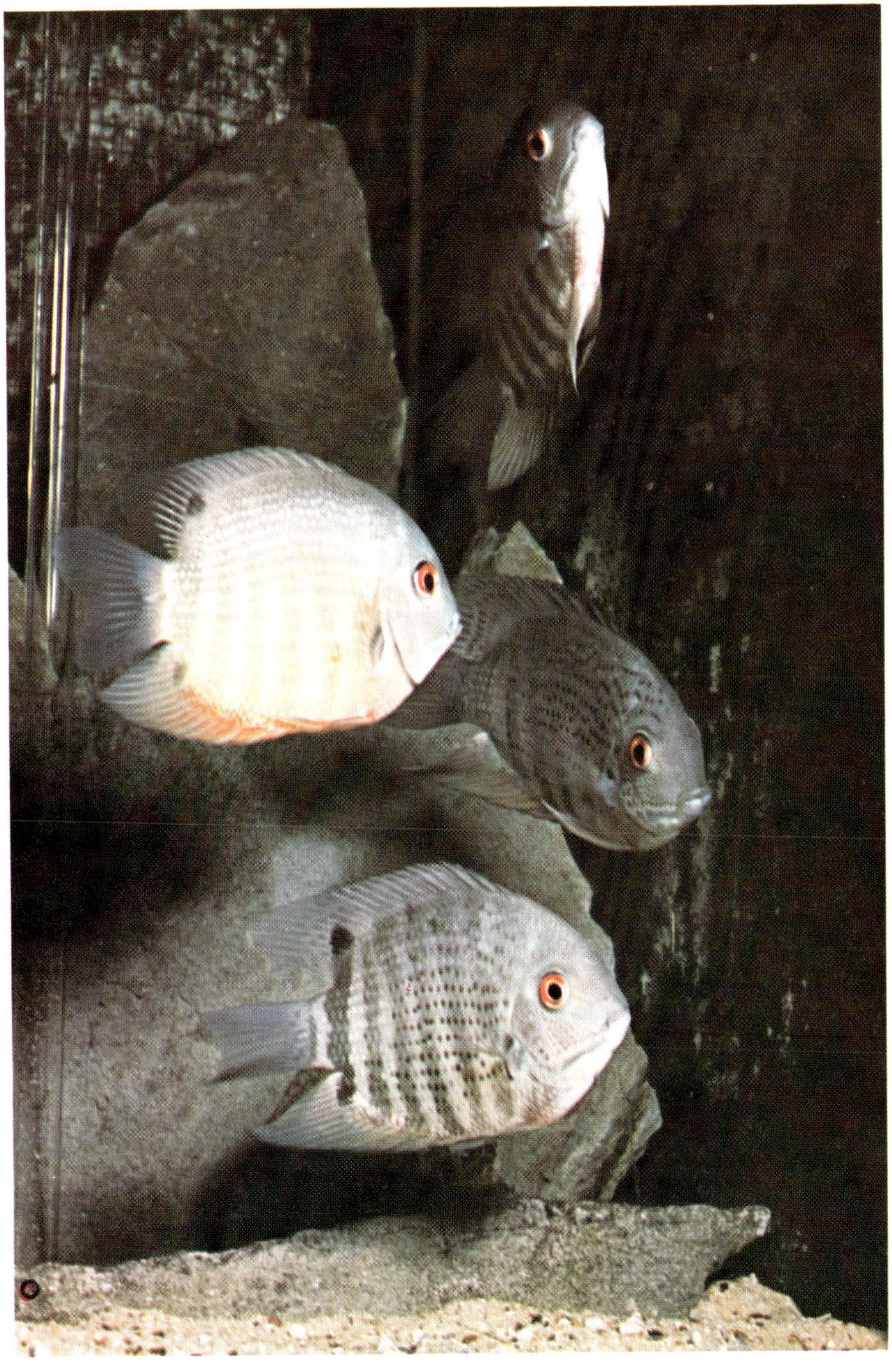

Discus or Pompadour

In its home territory in South America the discus is a favorite food of the Indians. The many varieties of discus, particularly the blue and the brown, are the pride of many aquarists. Although this fish is very beautiful, it is quite difficult to keep and breed. A large aquarium with decorative tree roots and large plants is necessary for its well-being. Soft, peaty water filtered crystal clear is one of the basic requirements for successful rearing of the discus. It must also be fed a varied diet of water fleas, red and white mosquito eggs, dragonfly's eggs, salt crabs, and insects. These fish are not sexually mature until two years, and then they lay their eggs on stones and plants. When hatched, the young attach themselves to plants by short threads, but they break free after two or three days. Then they fasten themselves to the parents' bodies which by this time have become dull and milky. The young fish seem to eat a sort of skin secretion given off by the parents.

Symphysodon discus comes from the Amazon River region. It grows up to 6 inches long and eats living food.

Water temperature: 77° to 80.6°F.

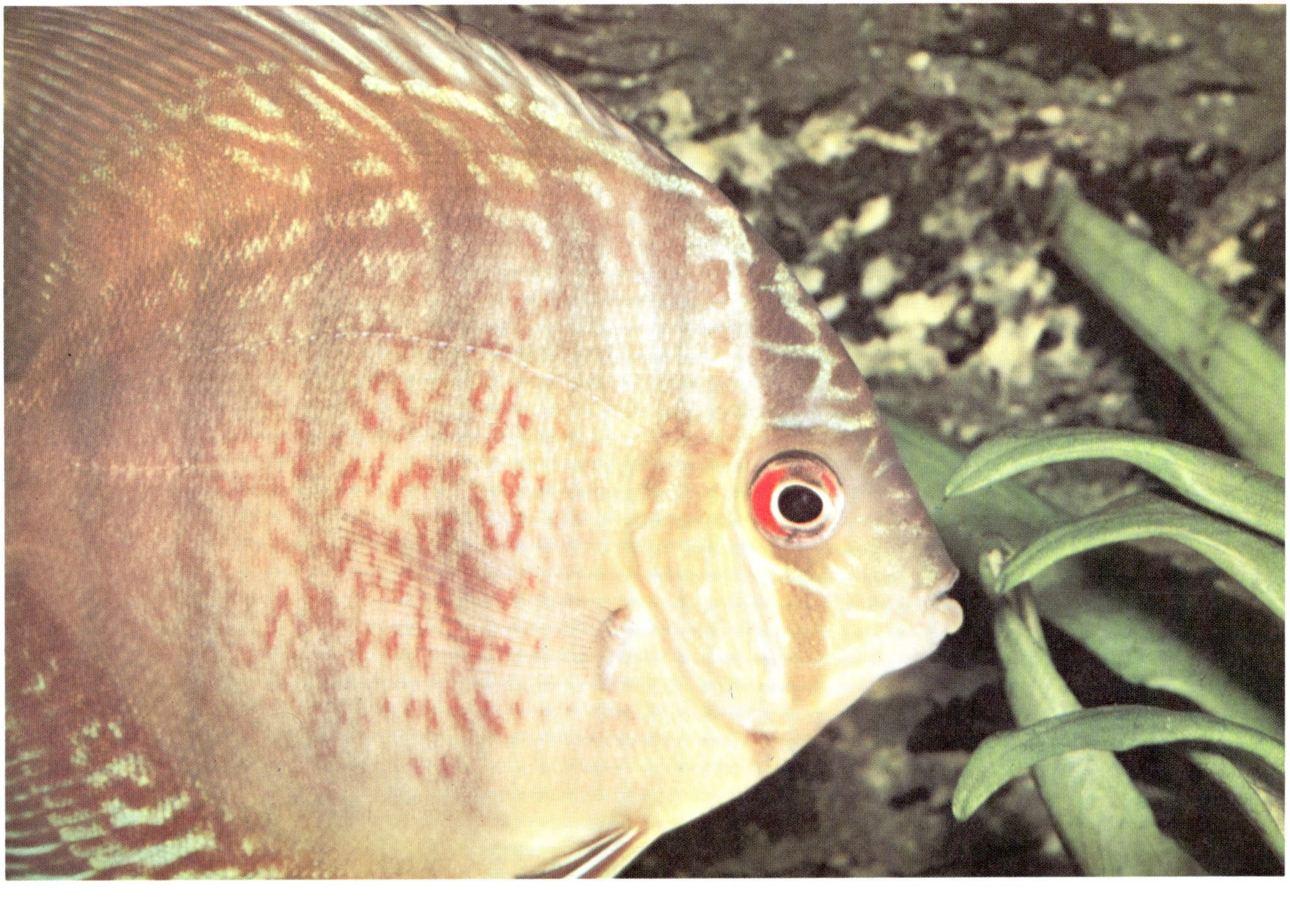

Angel Fish— young

In the family of large cichlids, the angel fish is among the few cichlids suitable for a mixed aquarium. Although it has a tendency to become nervous, it will remain peaceful if kept with other quiet fish species. Angel fish take great care of their young. Before the eggs are laid the parents carefully clean a large stone or a firm plant. The female then lays the eggs onto the stone or plant and the male fertilizes them. When the young hatch they are taken one by one into the mouth of the parents and carefully cleaned. Then they are spit out into a prepared hollow and moved again and again to a different place. The parents spend all their time caring for and protecting their young and scarcely eat during this period. After seven days the young swim freely in a group behind their parents. Our picture shows a young fish being spit from the parent's mouth after being cleaned.

Pterophyllum eimekei comes from the Amazon River region in South America. It grows up to 5 inches long and eats living and dried food.
Water temperature: 71.6° to 82.4°F.

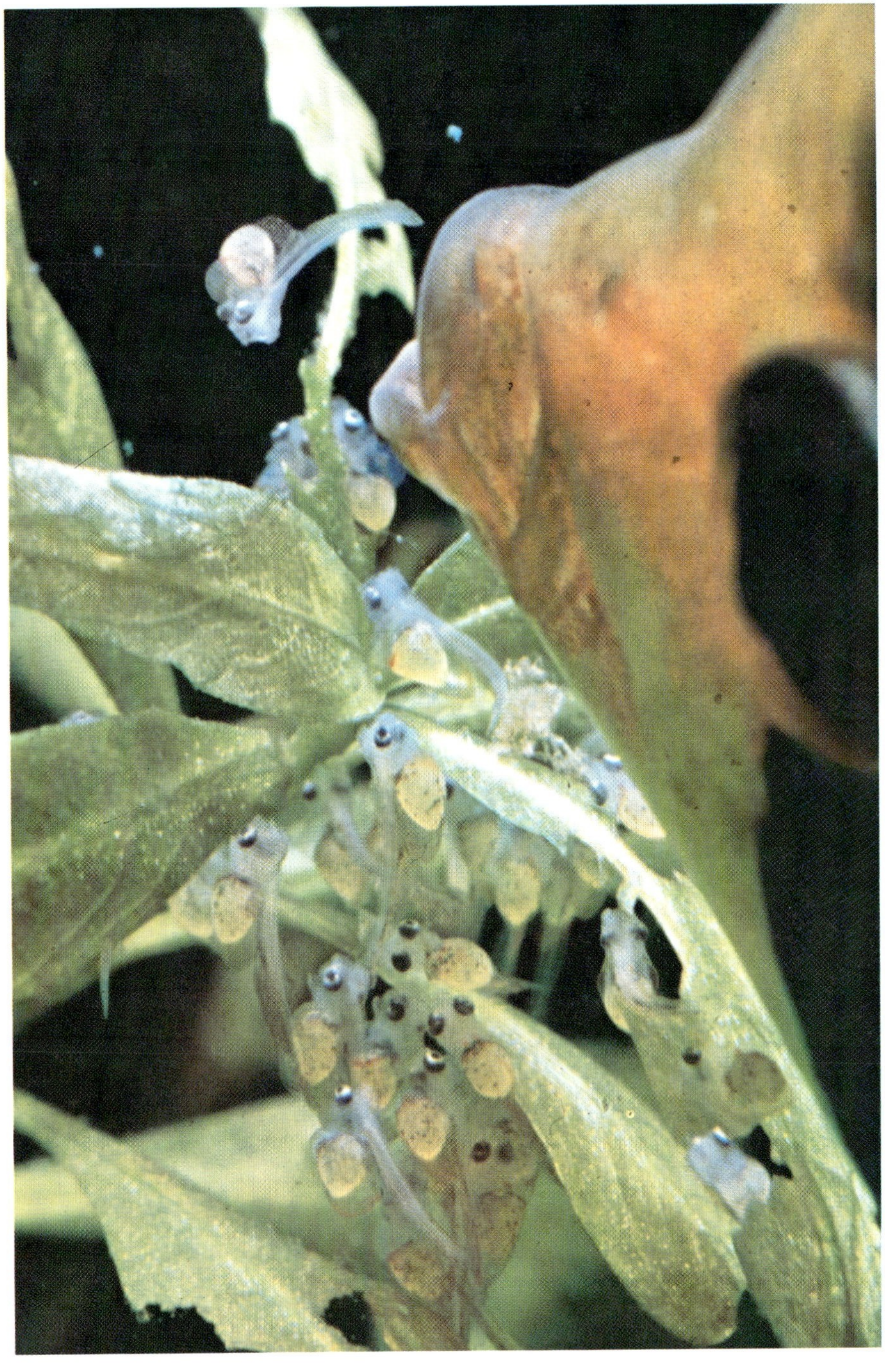

Paradise Fish

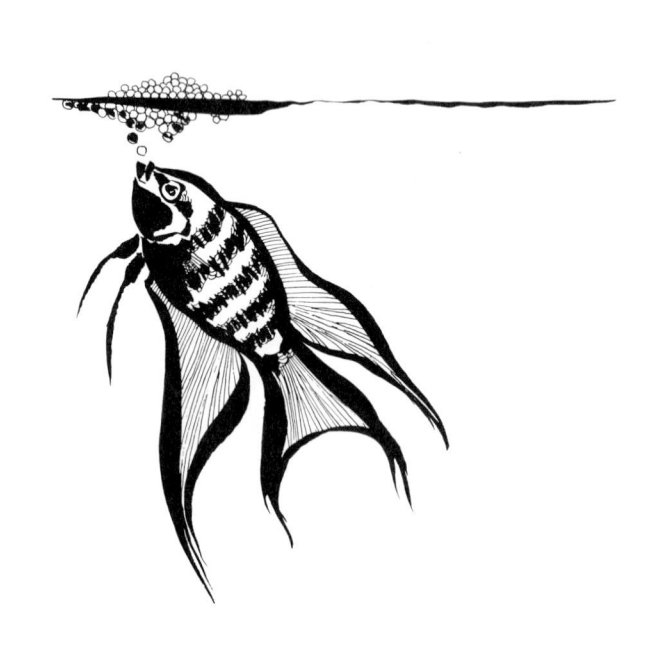

The paradise fish is a good fish for a beginner to keep in an unheated room aquarium because its habits make it an extremely interesting fish to observe. Before mating, the male builds a nest on the surface of the water. He does this by breathing in air, which he finally spits into the water as a bubble. He continues to make bubbles until the nest is 1/2 to 3/4 of an inch thick and has a diameter of about 2 inches. Then the male spreads his fins and swims after the female, showing off his finest colors. He entices the female under the nest where they do an intricate mating dance. Finally the couple embrace and the female lays the eggs. These are carefully collected by the male who spits them into the bubble nest. He then chases the female away, for it is the male's job to guard the nest and the eggs. He continually watches the nest and makes new bubbles to replace any that break. If any of the young fish try to leave the nest too early, he catches them in his mouth and carries them back. After several days the bubble nest disintegrates and the young swim around freely.

Macropodus opercularis comes from East Asia. It grows to 3 or 4 inches long and eats dried and living food.

Water temperature: 59° to 86°F.

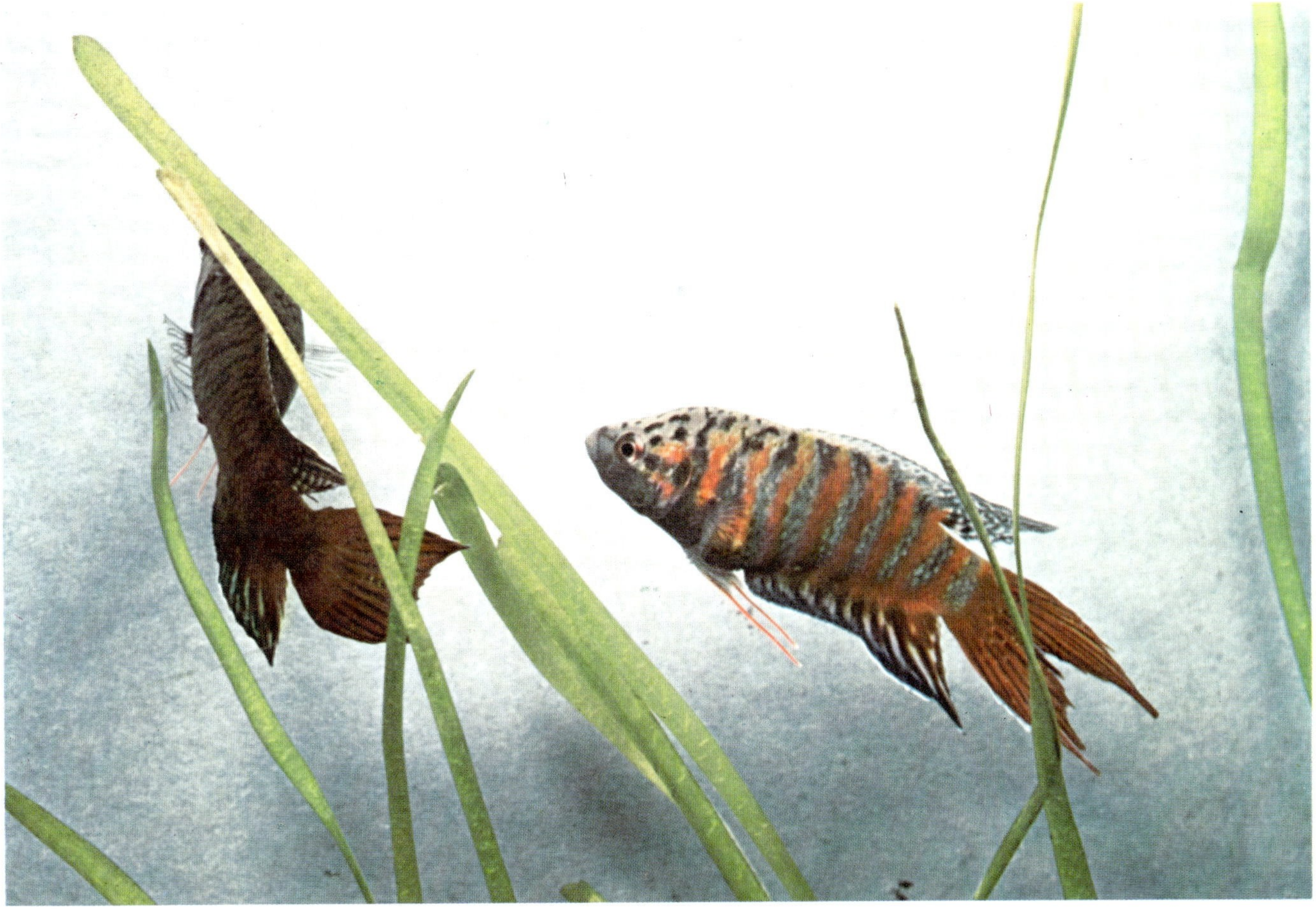

Siamese Fighting Fish

The people of modern Thailand hold fighting matches and beauty contests with male fighting fish. These contests are so popular that they are even taxed. In earlier years, when Thailand was called Siam, the Siamese experimented in the breeding of the male fighting fish in order to develop huge fins and a mixture of colors. As a result, males have been bred in colors of flesh pink, fiery red, emerald green, cornflower blue, and jet black, as well as all the combinations of these colors. The males are reared individually to aid the beautiful development of their fins, and they only meet other males in the fighting aquarium. In the arena they show their most beautiful colors and spread their fins almost to the tearing point. Then they dart at their opponent and try to tear his fins. Large bets are placed on these battles. After a long and furious struggle the losing fish is taken out so that the fight does not end with its death.

Betta splendens grows up to 2½ inches long and eats living and dried food.

Water temperature: 71.6° to 89.6°F.

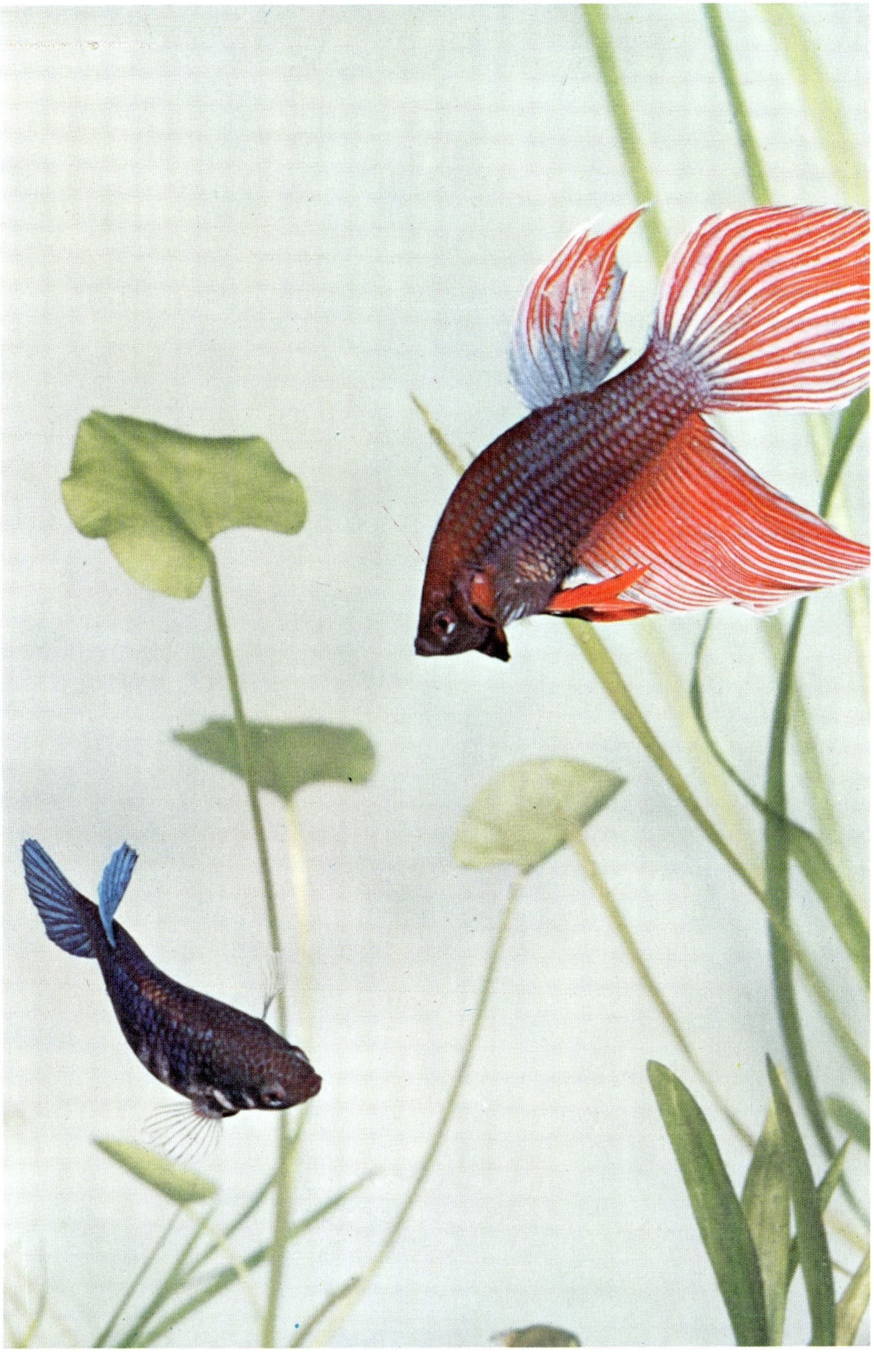

Three-spot Gourami

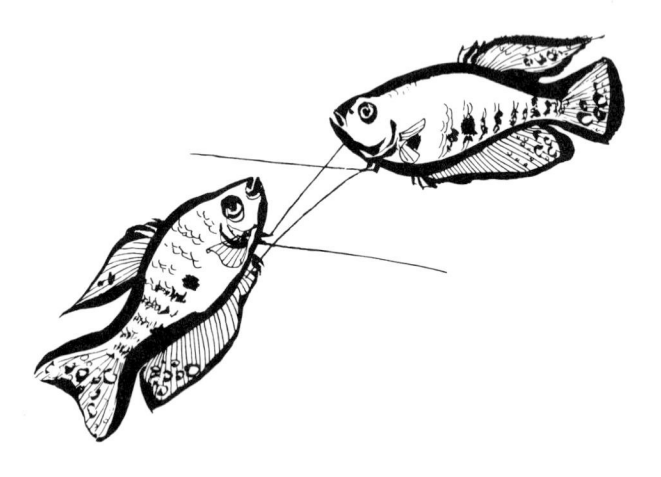

Blue is the dominant shade of this spotted gourami. Occasionally the males will become aggressive during the mating season, but gouramis are usually very peaceful fish. They glide slowly through the aquarium and feel out their area with their lengthened, threadlike belly fins. In the gourami species the organs of feeling, taste, and smell are contained in these threads, and the threads also act as eyes for the fish in the water. Their use of the threads can be observed when two gouramis meet. By looking closely you can see the feelers of each fish stretch forward and touch each other. Like many other fish, the gouramis' color varies a great deal. Their night color is completely different from their day color, which is a dark blue-black shade.

Trichogaster trichopterus sumatranus comes from Sumatra. It grows up to 5 inches long and eats dried and living food.

Water temperature: 75.2° to 82.4°F.

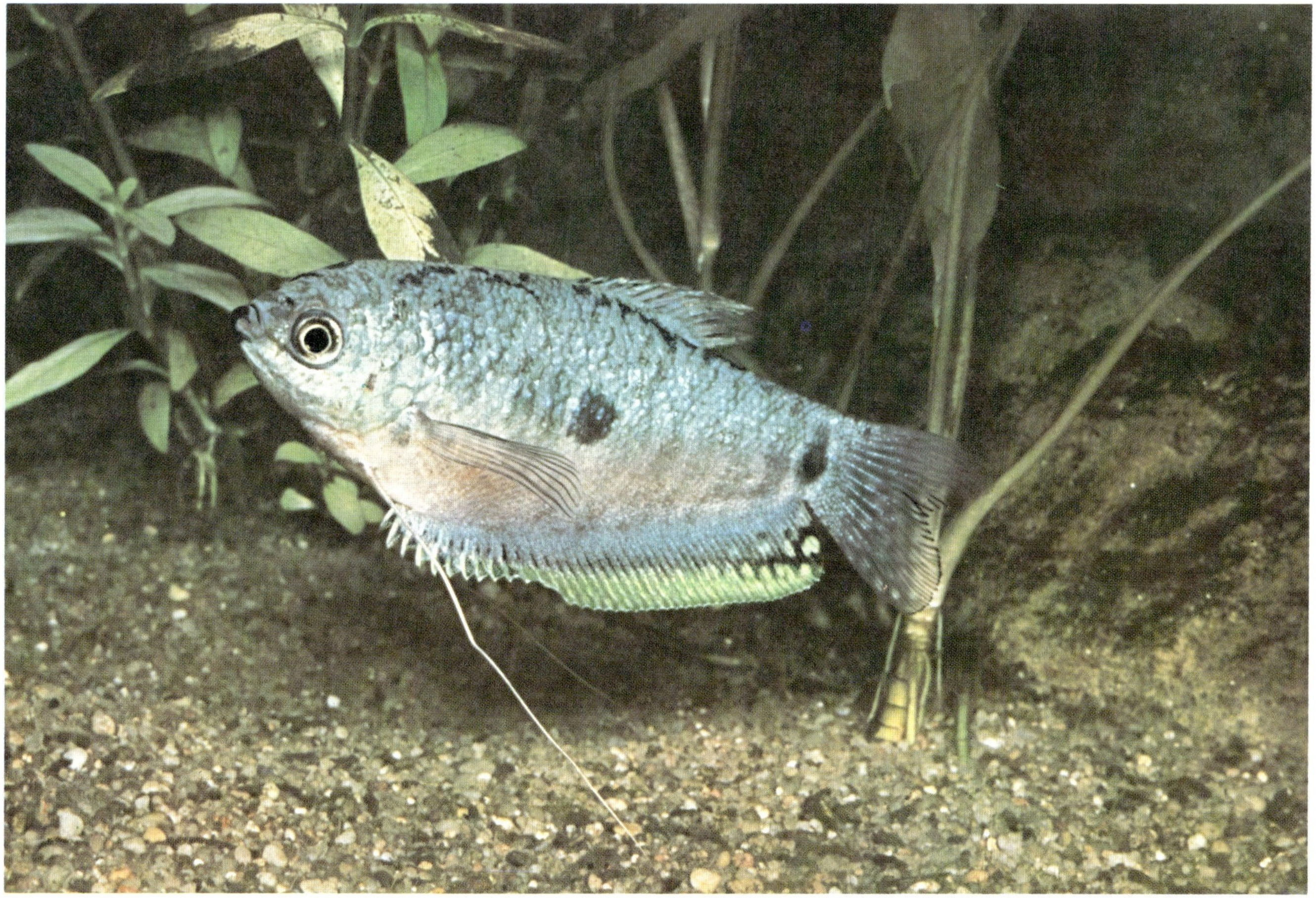

Lace Gourami

The lace gourami is the most difficult of the gourami to keep in an aquarium because it needs the right food and suitable plants for its full development. It is worth the trouble of keeping in an aquarium, however, because when it is full grown its mating colors are quite charming. The chest, the front part of the anal fin, and its two feelers are bright red, and the purple shimmering body makes its bright points shine out like precious stones. In contrast to the rough courtship of the fighting fish and the paradise fish, the loveplay of the lace gourami is especially tender. Its bubble nest is often deeper than 1¼ inches, and more than 3,000 eggs may be laid in it. When the lace gourami finds its aquarium suitable it develops its most beautiful colors and looks like a jewel among the other aquarium fish.

Trichogaster leeri comes from India and Indonesia. It grows up to 4 inches long and eats dried and living food.

Water temperature: 75.2° to 86°F.

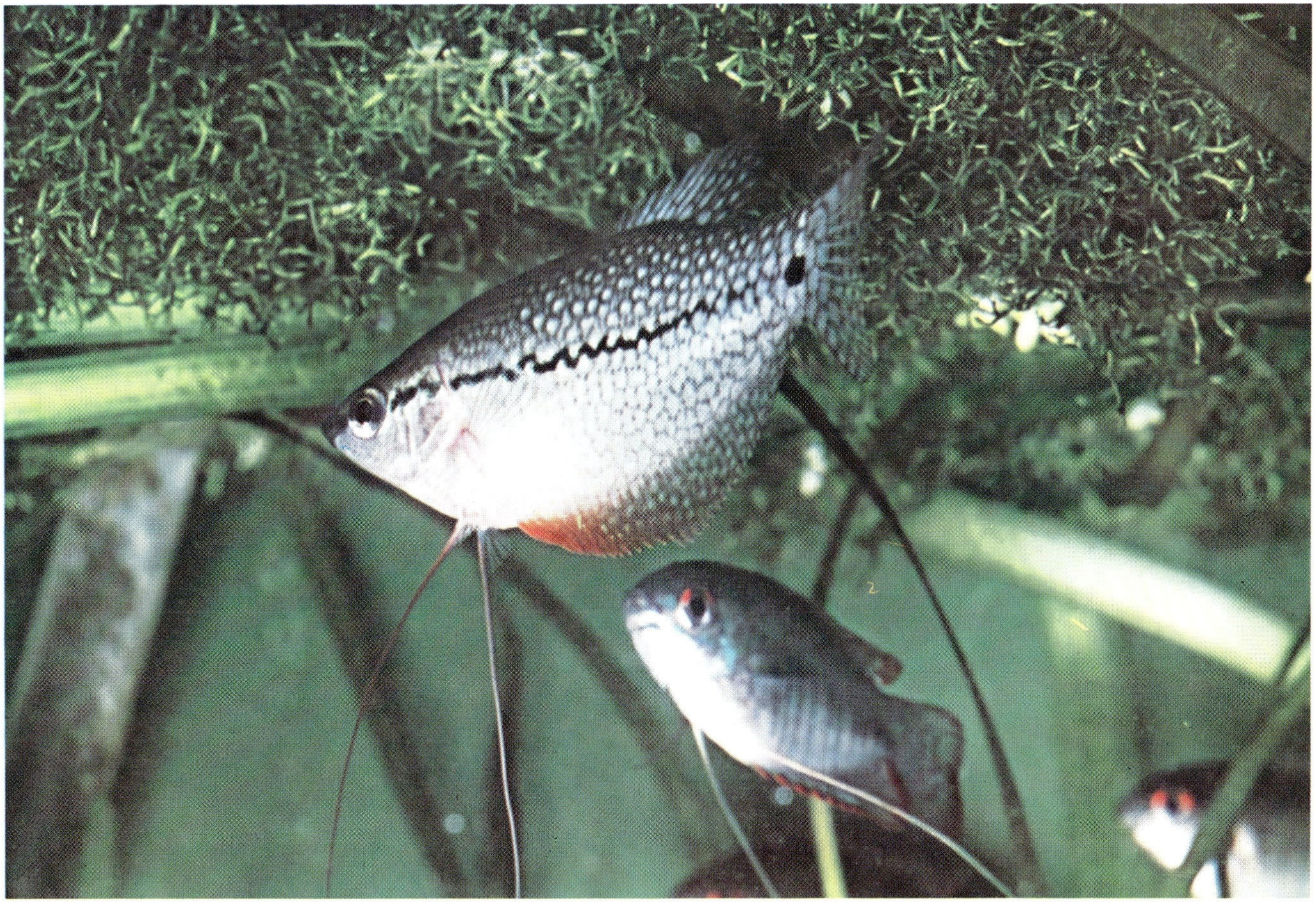

Dwarf Gourami

The dwarf gourami is one of the most beautiful of the aquarium fish. Its natural setting is the muddy rice field, but in captivity it seems to prefer sunny aquariums that have an abundance of wild plants. Most fish need to live in water containing plenty of oxygen, but the labyrinth family (to which the gouramis, the fighting fish, the paradise fish, and the climbing fish belong) do not. This is because they have completely adapted to the unusual conditions in their natural home. The rice fields become warmed so quickly by the sun that the oxygen content of the water rapidly drops, and the fish must depend on another way of getting the oxygen they need. The gourami has the gill system common to most fish through which it takes in oxygen from the water, and it also has a skin pouch on either side of the gills. These pouches have deep furrows in them. The mucous membrane in the furrows contains blood that can take in the oxygen that the fish breathes from the air on the water surface. It is possible that a labyrinth fish kept away from the surface of the water could actually drown.

Colisa lalia comes from India. It is 2 inches long and eats dried and living food.

Water temperature: 75.2° to 89.6°F.

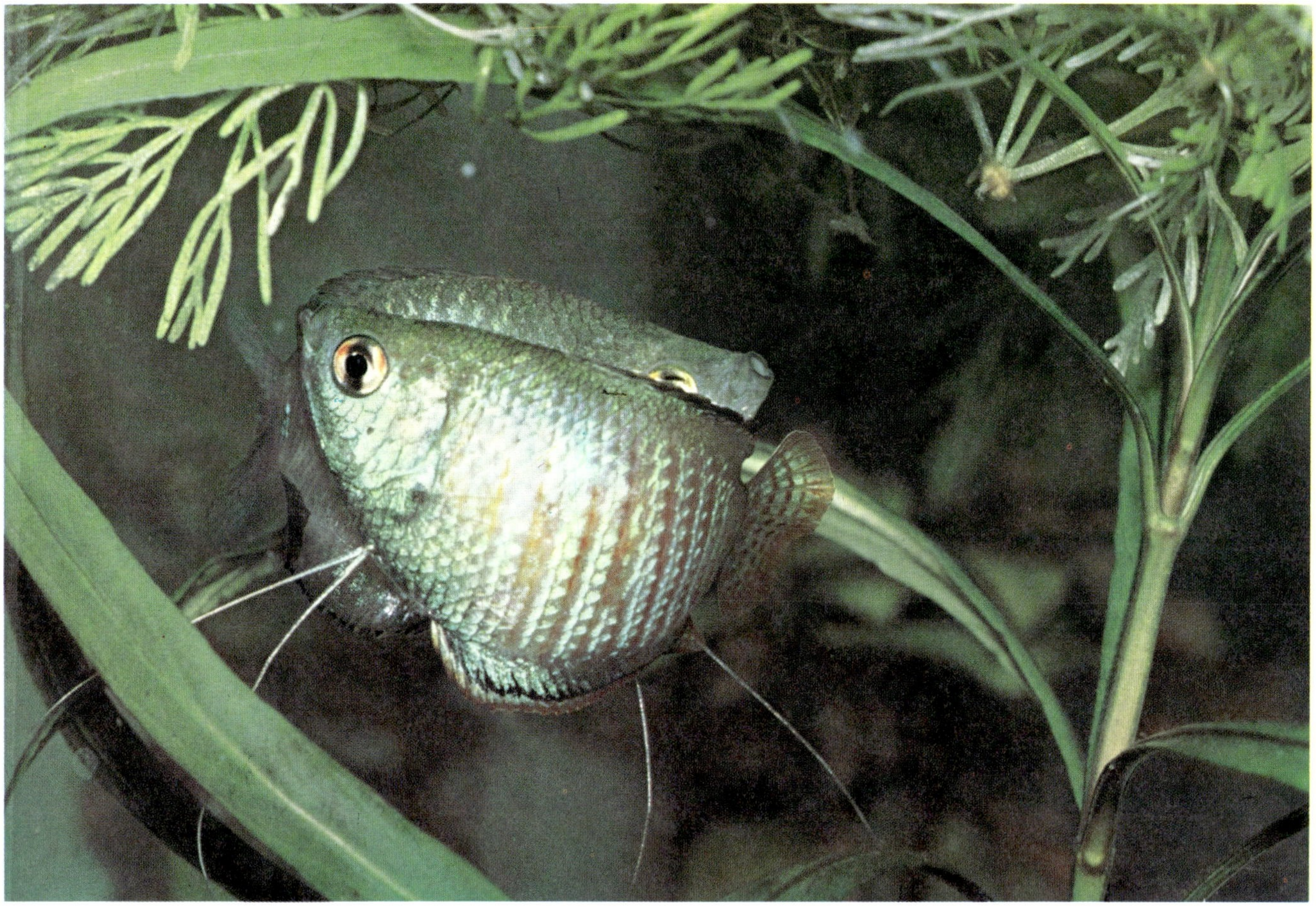

Diagonal Swimmer or Penguin Fish

Although this fish variety is not distinguished by any intense coloring, its marking makes it a striking member of the mixed aquarium. A large shoal of these fish make quite an interesting picture, for they like to swim in a diagonal position. A black line stretches down the diagonal swimmer's body and bends at the bottom end of the tail fin. This makes the line of its diagonal position seem steeper than it really is. Diagonal swimmers are peaceful fish and love a well-planted aquarium. The breeding of these fish is not easy work. The soft-water temperature must be at 82.4°F. The parents like to lay their eggs between plants near the bottom in an aquarium made completely of glass; they will lay up to 1,000 eggs. After the egg-laying is completed the water should be partly removed and the parents taken out because they eat their own eggs. The young fish swim freely after five days.

Thayeria boehlkei comes from the Amazon River region. It grows up to 3 inches long and will eat every kind of fish food available.

Water temperature: 73.4° to 82.4°F.

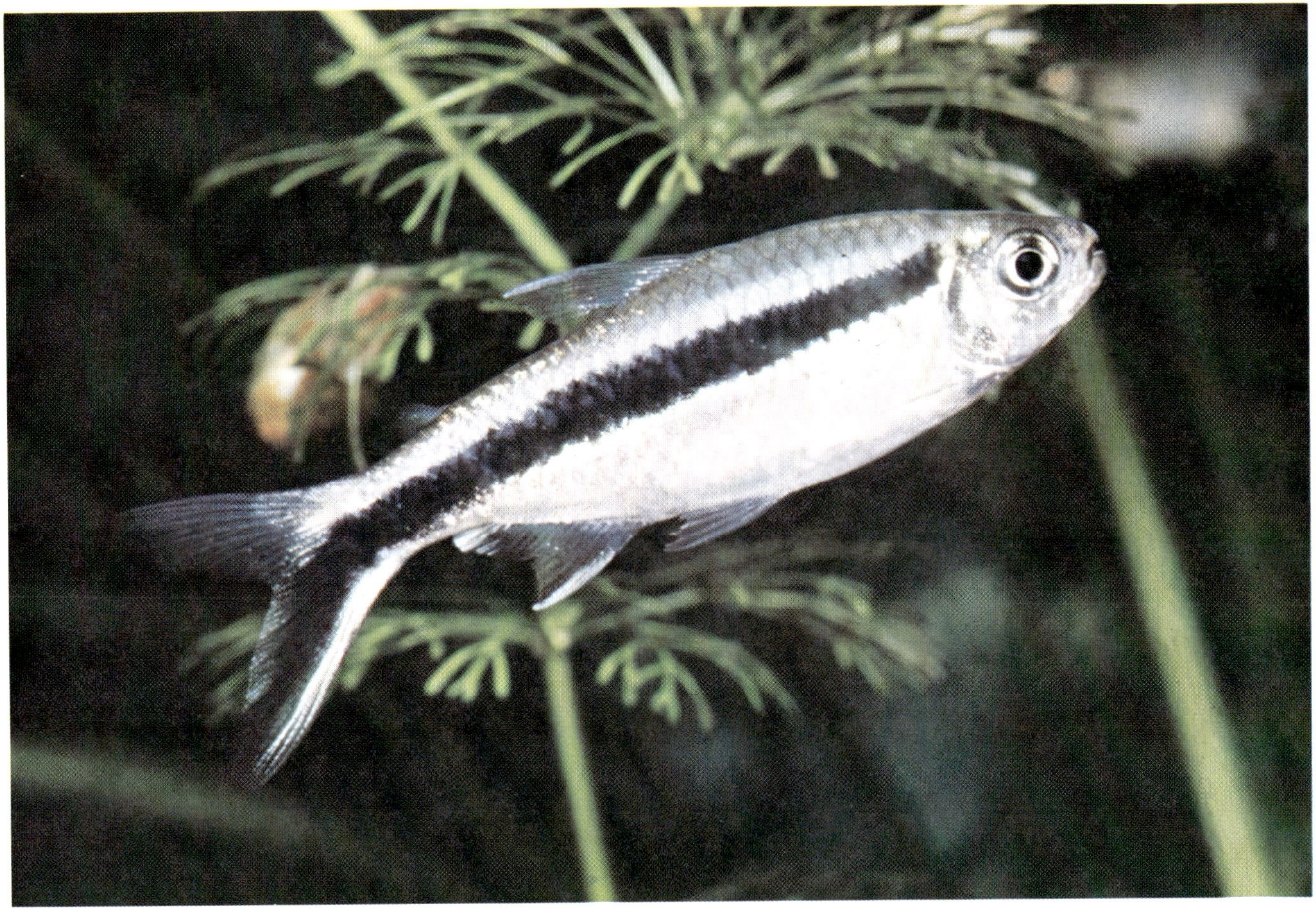

Serpae Tetra

Although this fish is often called the serpae tetra, tropical fish experts have been arguing about its classification for years. Its name is questioned because the serpae tetra has not been imported for a long time, and some people claim that it was never imported at all. The different forms of this species vary in their stages of growth from having a very definite shoulder spot to having no spot at all. As a result, the grouping of them as varieties or sub-varieties has not been decided. The intensity of its red coloring also varies considerably in different breeds. The serpae tetra prefers a large aquarium with plenty of room for free swimming and good hiding places among the plants. During breeding the couples follow each other gaily through the water plants, where they lay and fertilize their eggs.

Hyphessobrycon callistus callistus (serpae) comes from South America. It grows up to 1½ inches long and eats dried and living food.

Water temperature: 73.4° to 82.4°F.

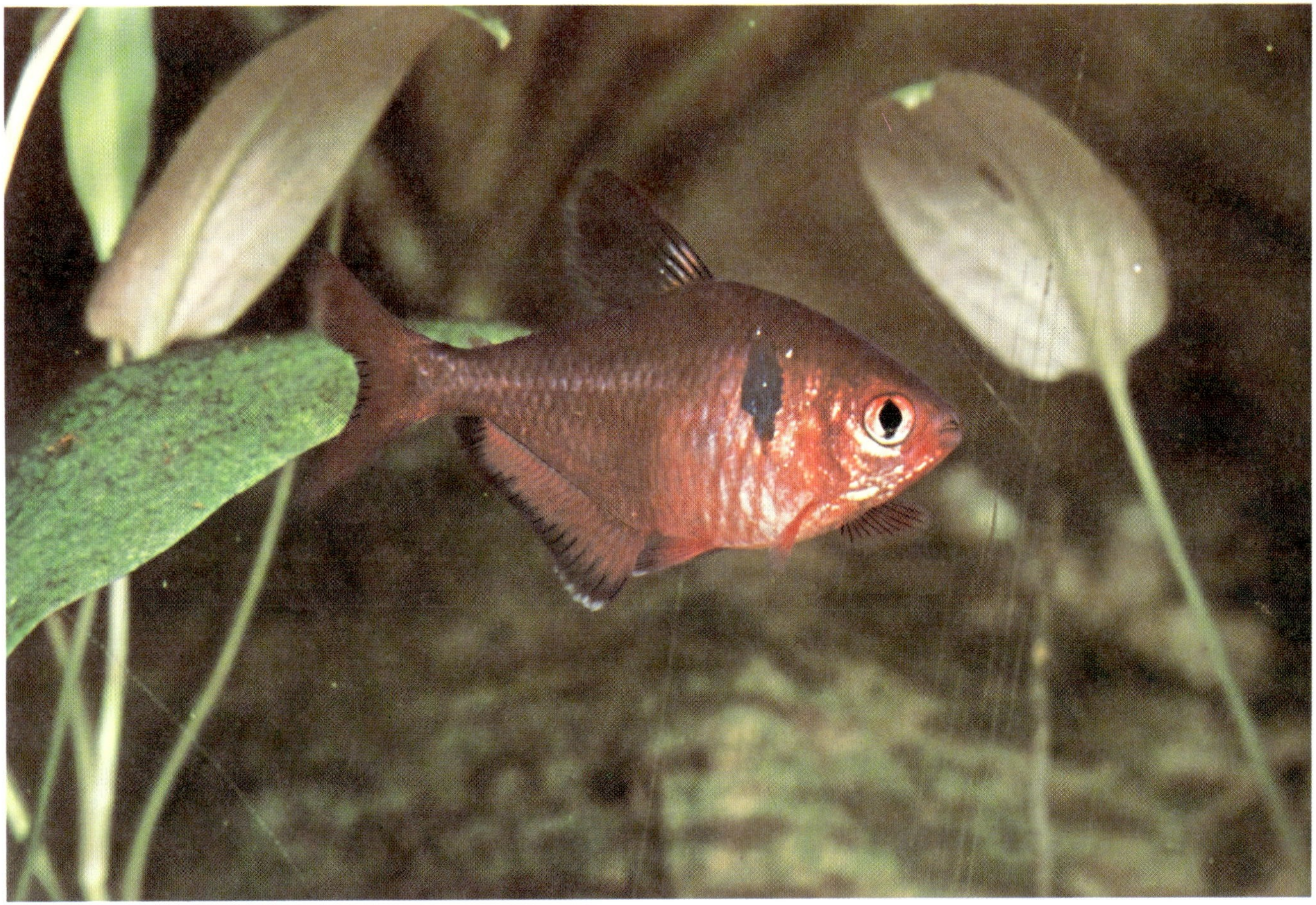

Flame Fish or Flame Tetra

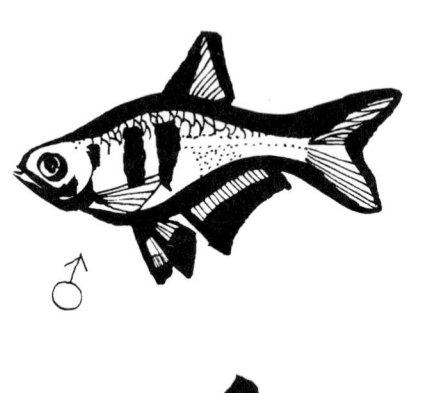

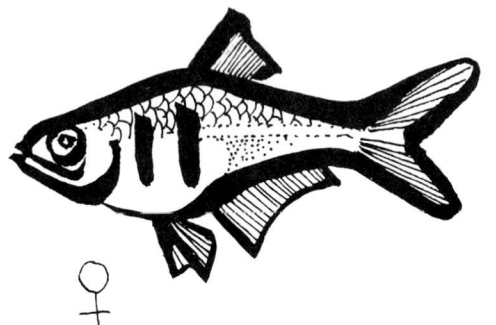

The flame tetra is a fish easily raised by a beginner because it can exist in an unheated room aquarium. It needs warmer water temperatures in order to develop its full colors, however. The male and female flame tetras are difficult to distinguish from each other, but the females are usually a little larger and fuller than the males, and the males have black-edged anal fins. It is sometimes not possible to tell if one has a pair of male and female tetras until young fish have actually hatched from the eggs that were laid. This is because two females together will often behave like a normal pair of male and female fish. Both females will lay eggs, but because the eggs have not been fertilized by a male, young fish will not hatch from them. The flame tetra is easy to breed, however, and is very productive.

Hyphessobrycon flammeus comes from the Rio de Janeiro area of Brazil. It is approximately 1½ inches long and eats dried and living food.

Water temperature: 68° to 75.2°F.

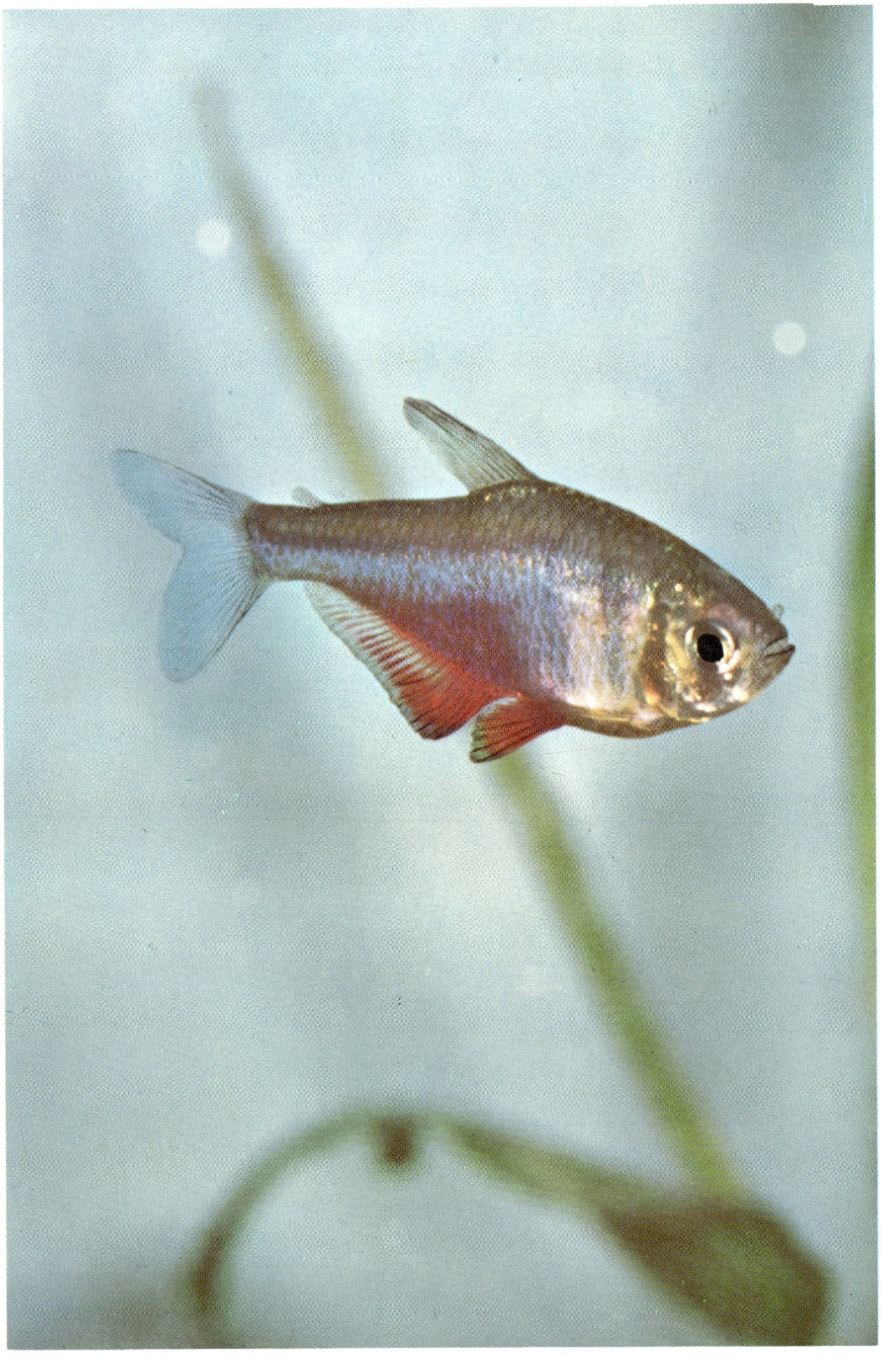

X-ray Fish

The x-ray fish has strong colors of black, yellow, and red. Its coloring is very similar to that of the goldfinch bird, and because of this the x-ray fish is sometimes called the water goldfinch. It is also called a star-spotted tetra because of the distinctive yellow-edged spot on its dorsal fin. In South America the x-ray fish lives in large shoals in small water areas. In captivity it only develops its full colors when kept in a well-planted aquarium in water of medium temperature. Fine-leaved plants suit its environment very well. When the fish feels contented, his shining red tail fin and the yellow edges around the black spots on the dorsal and anal fins are very noticeable. If the x-ray fish does not like something its colors fade completely. The males and females look very much alike but they can be distinguished from each other if seen in a bright light. The end of the body cavity on the male is pointed and more rounded than on the female.

Pristella riddlei comes from the northern part of South America. It grows up to 2 inches long and eats dried and living food.

Water temperature: 68° to 78.8°F.

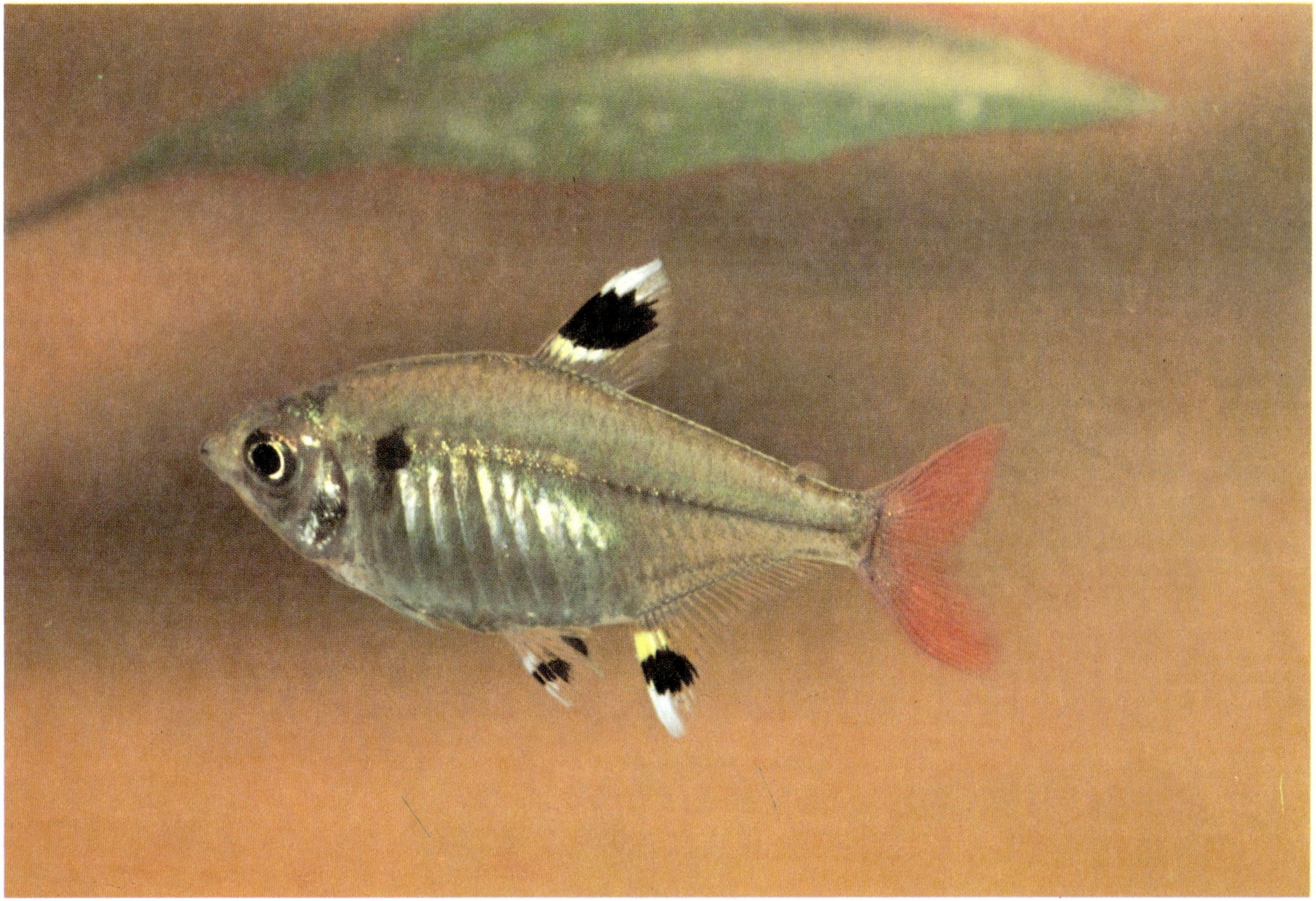

Ornate or Rosy Tetra

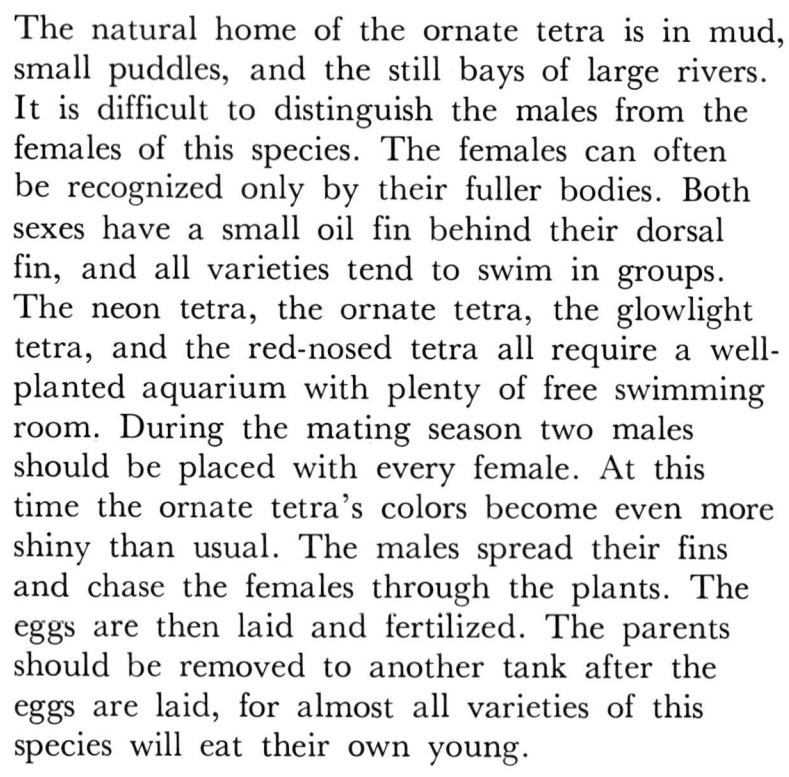

The natural home of the ornate tetra is in mud, small puddles, and the still bays of large rivers. It is difficult to distinguish the males from the females of this species. The females can often be recognized only by their fuller bodies. Both sexes have a small oil fin behind their dorsal fin, and all varieties tend to swim in groups. The neon tetra, the ornate tetra, the glowlight tetra, and the red-nosed tetra all require a well-planted aquarium with plenty of free swimming room. During the mating season two males should be placed with every female. At this time the ornate tetra's colors become even more shiny than usual. The males spread their fins and chase the females through the plants. The eggs are then laid and fertilized. The parents should be removed to another tank after the eggs are laid, for almost all varieties of this species will eat their own young.

Hyphessobrycon ornatus comes from South America. It is 1½ inches long and eats dried and living food.

Water temperature: 73.4° to 82.4°F.

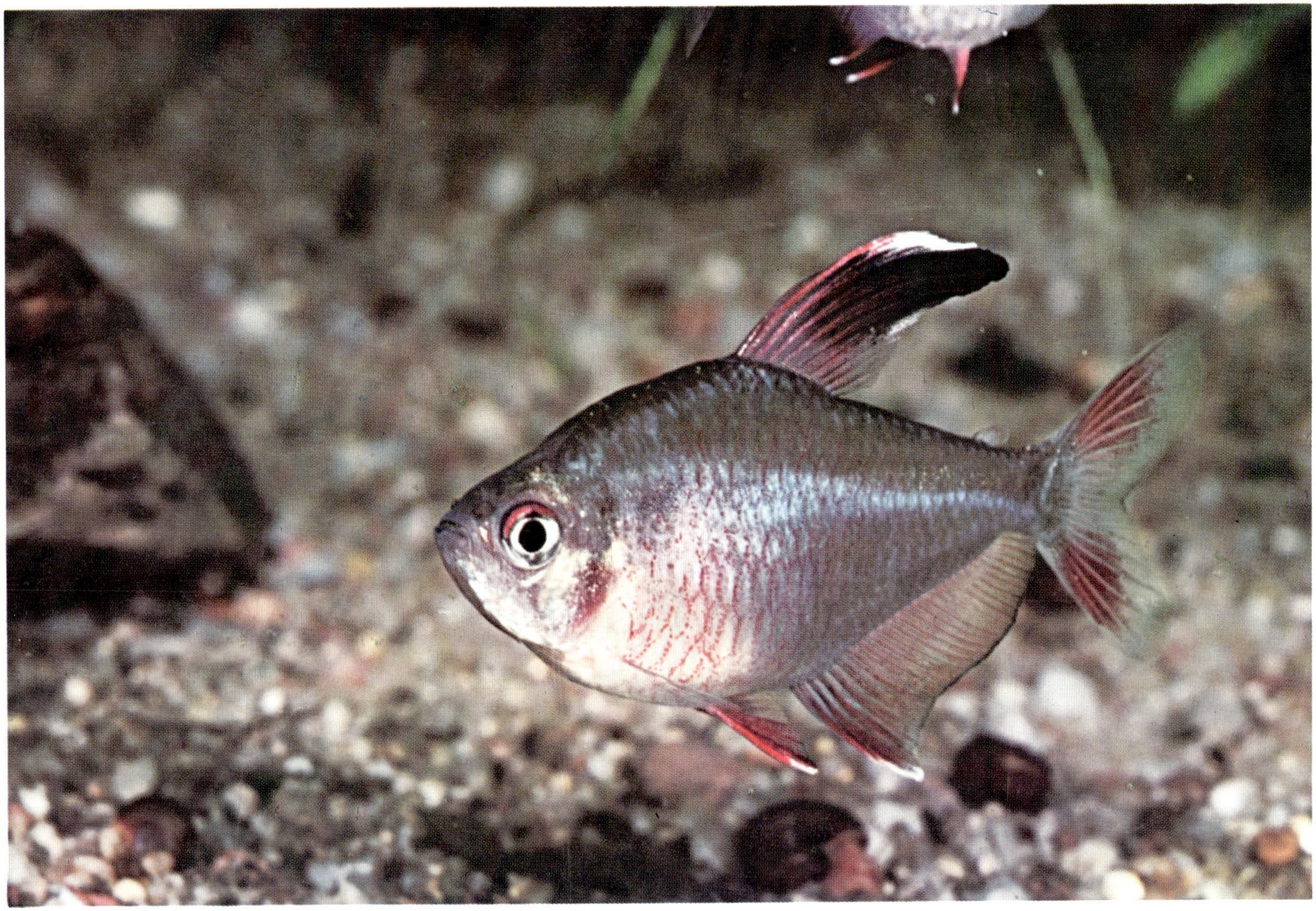

Glowlight Tetra

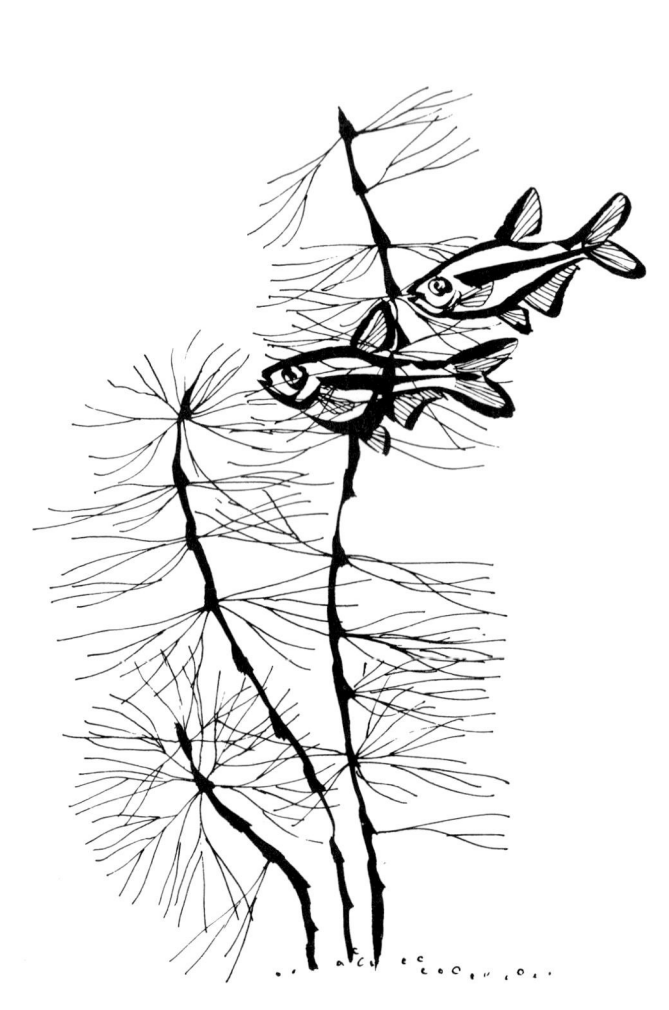

This fish comes from the woodland lakes of South America and needs a warmer water temperature than do others of its species. The male and the female glowlight tetras are easy to distinguish from each other. The females are strong and round. The males are smaller than the females and have a sunken body. The mating procedure of the glowlight tetra is very charming. The fish swim among thick plants, sometimes while lying on their sides or even on their backs. The young fish hatch 24 days after the eggs are laid and grow quickly if fed well on living food of fine quality. The shimmering red stripes along the body of the glowlight tetra shine among the green of the aquarium plants. The fish only develop their proper activity in normal-sized groups. The more fish there are in a shoal, the more active is their play and the more beautiful are their colors. All tetras should be kept in shoals of 8 to 10 fish for only then do they find suitable partners for mating.

Hemigrammus erythrozonus comes from South America. It grows up to 1½ inches long and eats living and dried food.

Water temperature: 75.2° to 82.4°F.

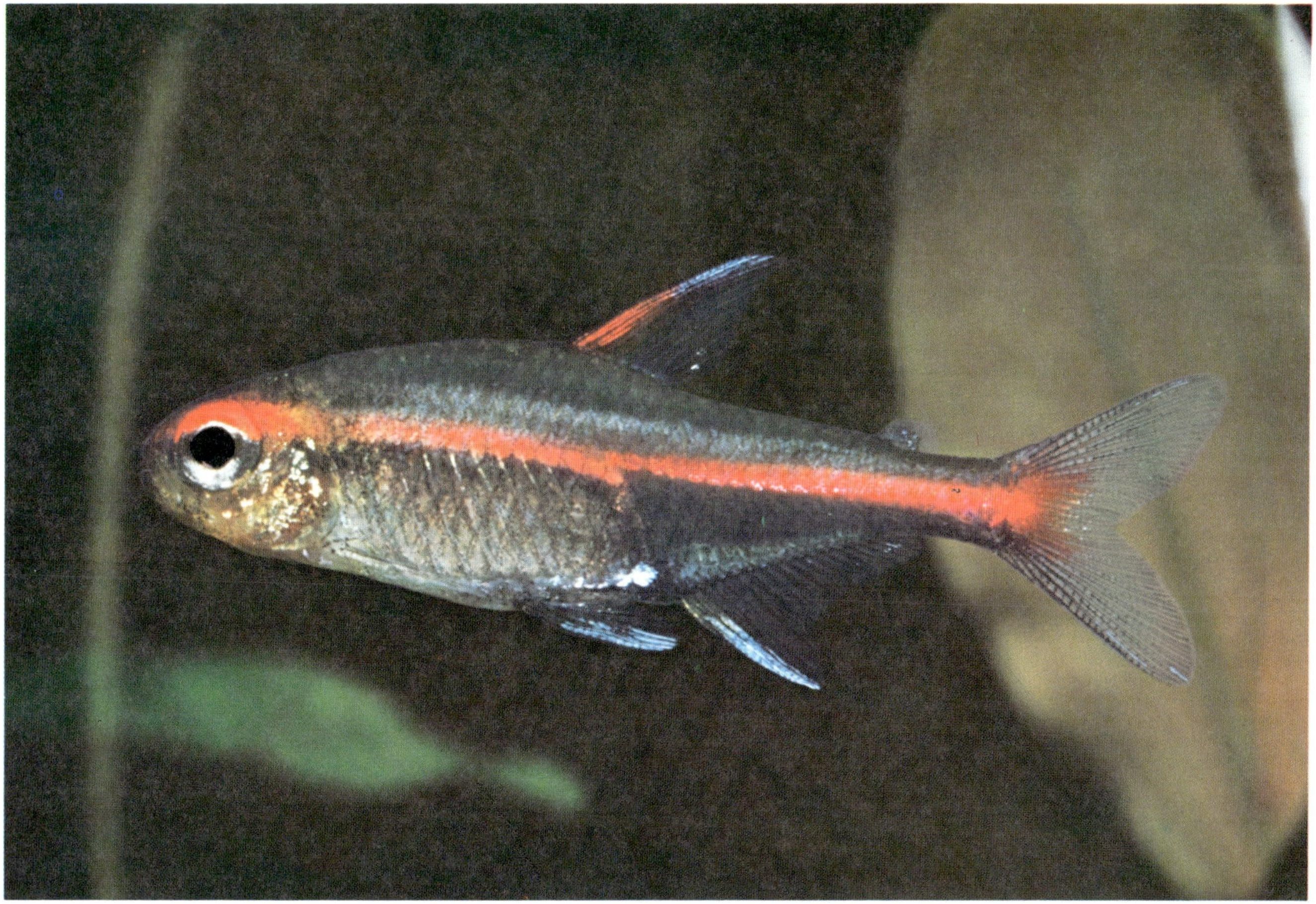

Neon Tetra

In 1936 one of the most beautiful of the aquarium fish was imported to other countries from its home in the region of the upper Amazon River. The neon tetra has a shining blue line running the entire length of its body. This line takes on varying shades of blue depending on the light. Like many tetras this fish lives in large shoals. Once it becomes used to the aquarium the neon tetra will live with other peaceful fish for a long time. It is a pleasant fish to keep because it is not particular about water temperature and food. It can easily be fed dried food and water fleas. Young neons must never be mixed with angel fish because angel fish find the color combination of the neon tetra so appealing that they will try to eat it. If the aquarist wishes to keep both fish together, young angel fish should be introduced into a group of settled adult neons.

Hyphessobrycon innesi comes from the Amazon River region. It grows to almost 1½ inches long and eats living and dried food.

Water temperature: 68° to 75.2°F.

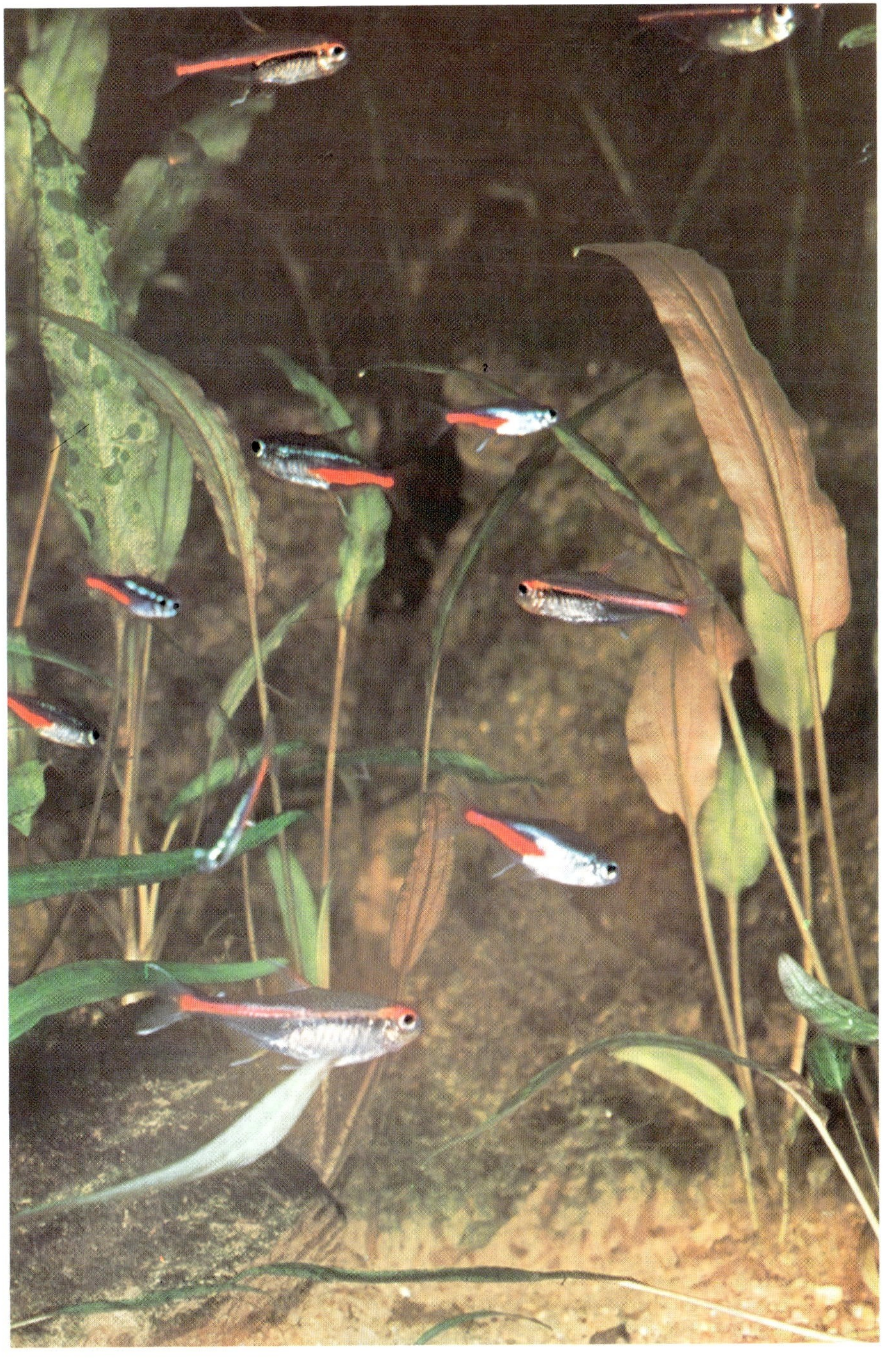

Cardinal Tetra

Since the discovery of the cardinal tetra in 1956, aquarists have disagreed about whether it is a more beautiful tropical fish than the neon tetra. The cardinal tetra belongs to a closely related subfamily of the neon tetra, but there are varying opinions about its specific classification. The two fish are so similar in their mating habits that it is easy to crossbreed them. The cardinal tetra needs very soft water for breeding. Its eggs and hatched young should be kept in shaded water. The young fish grow slowly and do not become sexually mature until the age of 9 or 10 months. Although it is fairly easy to keep the cardinal tetra, only experienced aquarists manage to breed them because these fish are very particular about choosing their mates.

Hyphessobrycon Cardinalis also known as *Cheirodon axelrodi* comes from the waters of the Rio Negro in South America. It grows up to 1½ inches long and eats dried and living food.

Water temperature: 69.8° to 77°F.

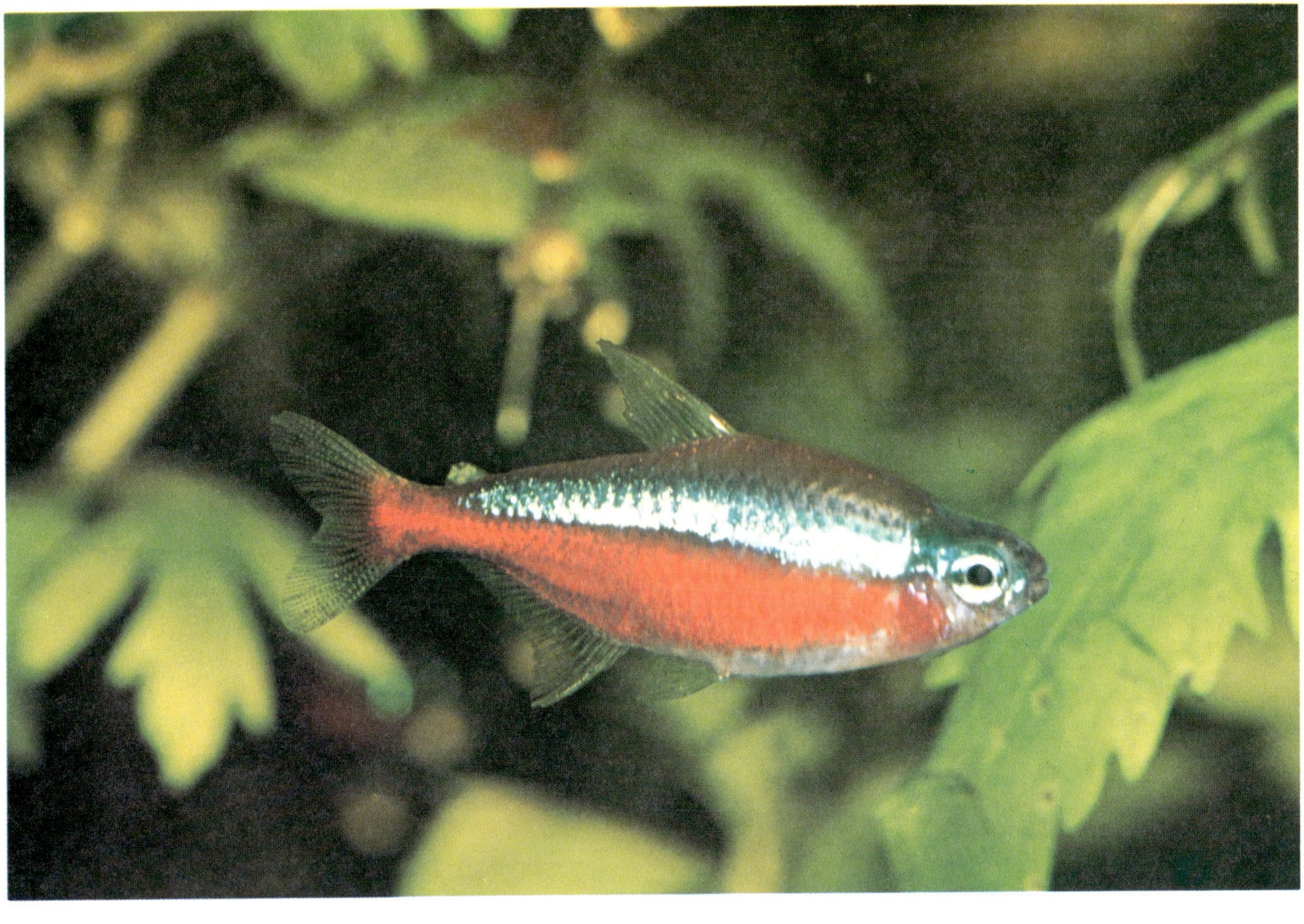

Red-nosed Tetra

Most fish do not reach their most beautiful stage until they are fully grown and do not develop their brightest colors until mating time. It is recommended that the aquarist buy fish when they are young and plainly colored, for then he can watch them develop into beautiful adult fish in his own aquarium. Another reason for buying young fish is that the adult fish cannot settle in a new home as quickly as the younger fish and often become homesick for their old surroundings. In most cases the good care of fish will result in their quick growth, which is usually noticeable after six months. A varied diet and a great deal of living food are necessary for the full development of most fish. This is especially true of the red-nosed tetra; it develops its red nose rather late and may never show this color if it does not have suitable food and surroundings.

Hemigrammus rhodostomus comes from the Amazon River region. It grows up to 1½ inches long and eats dried and living food.

Water temperature: 73.4° to 77°F.

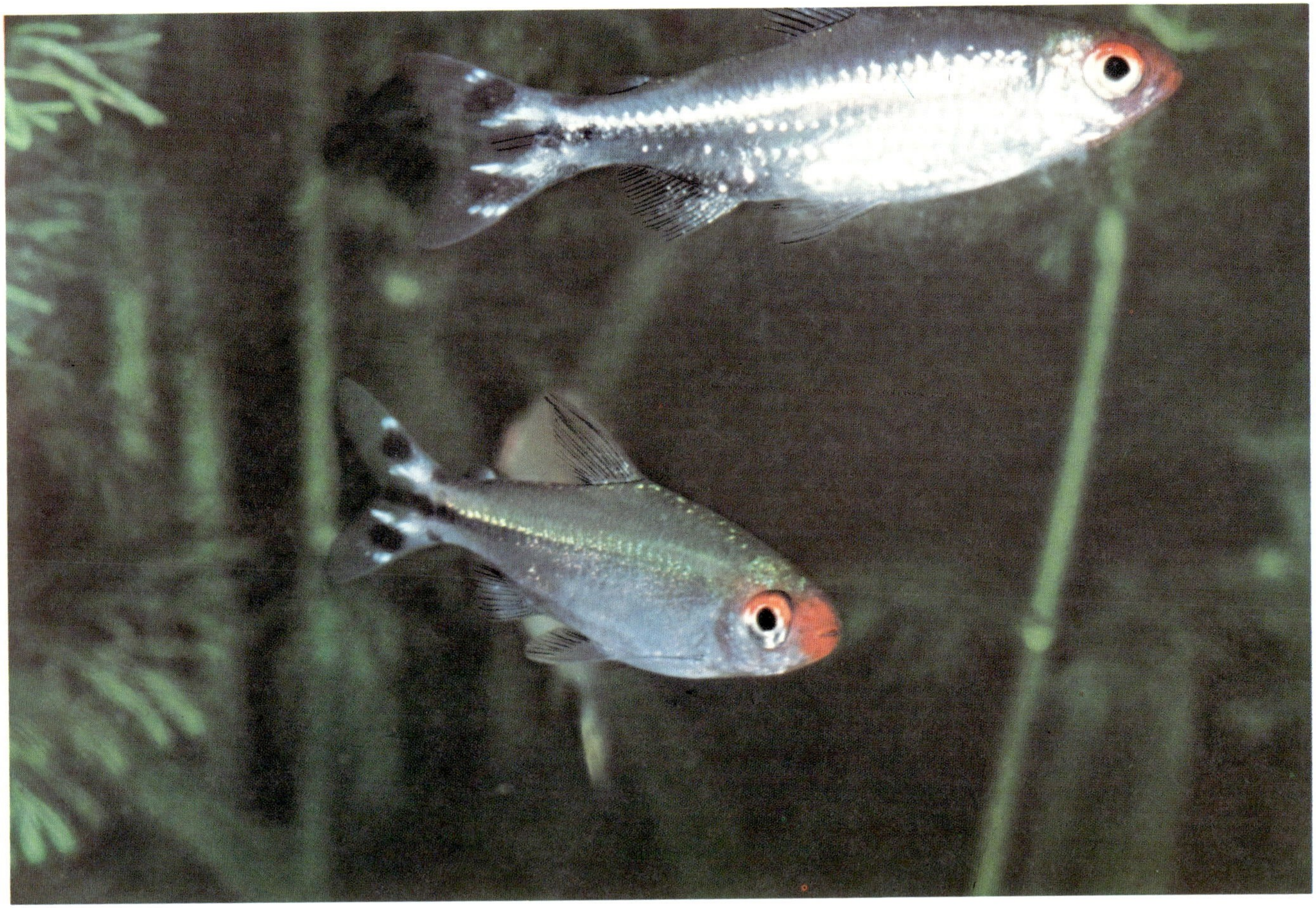

Congo Tetra

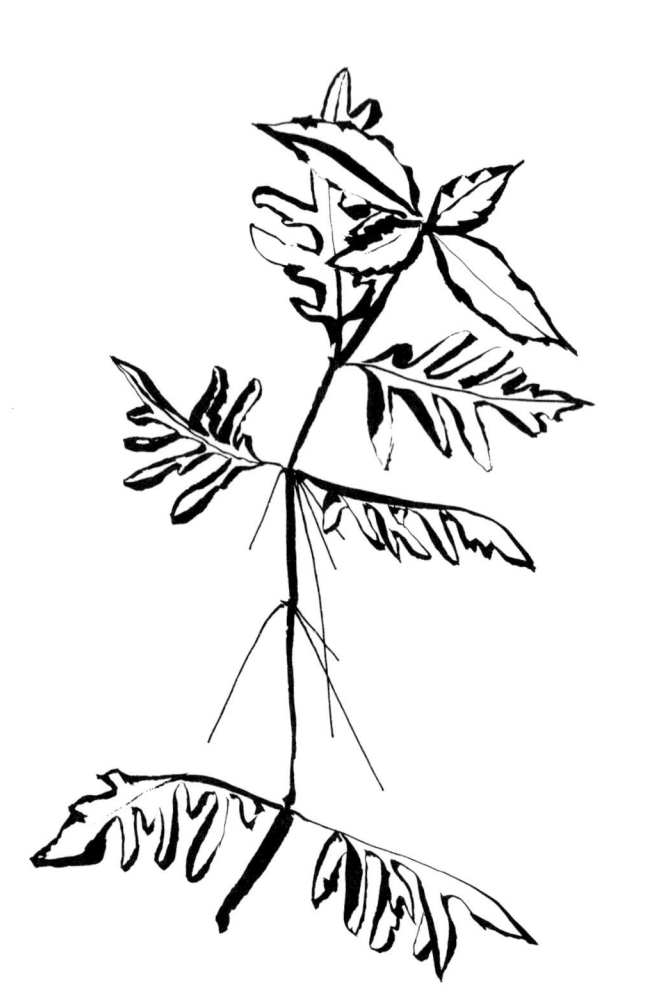

The colorful tetras of South America have relatives just as colorful in the region of the Congo River in Africa. One of these is the congo tetra which shines in all the colors of the rainbow. It was not discovered until 1949, and aquarists are still trying to breed it successfully. Unfortunately, the beauty of this fish diminishes with breeding. The extended central part of the tail fin is seldom found in sub-breeds, but the reasons for this are still not clear. The congo tetra is greatly influenced by the water composition of the aquarium, and should be kept in soft water that has been filtered through peat and is slightly sour. The shining blue central part of the male's tail fin which is normally 3/4 inches long and 1/16 inches wide can disappear overnight if the condition of the water becomes unsuitable to the fish. It will only grow again to its former beauty very slowly if the fish is placed in better water.

Micralestes (Phenacogrammus) interruptus comes from the Congo. It grows up to 2½ inches long and eats dried and living food.

Water temperature: 73.4° to 77°F.

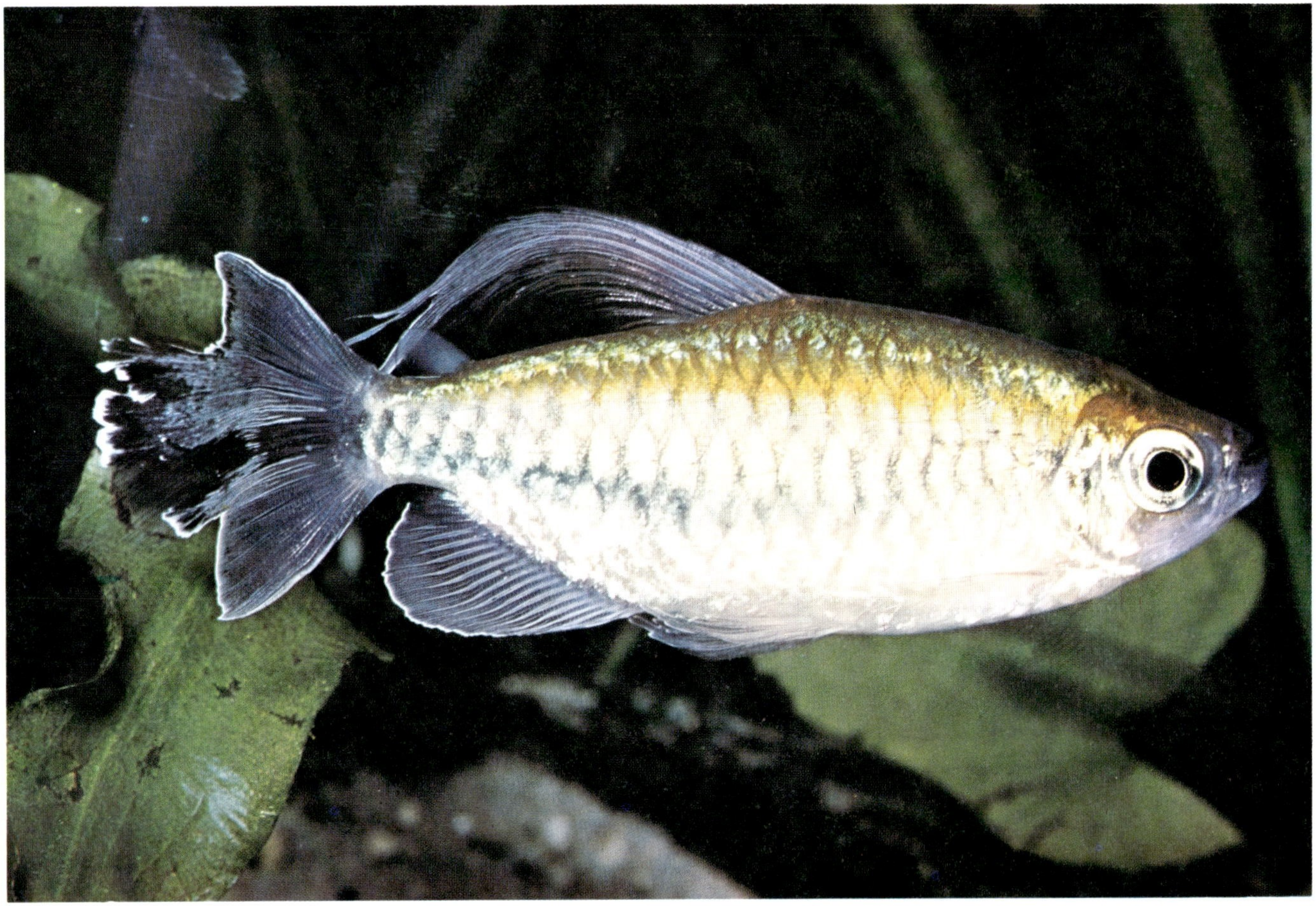

NATURE AND MAN

Other Books in This Series

AMONG THE PLAINS INDIANS, a fictional account based on the actual travels of two explorers who observed American Indian life in the 1830's, features illustrations by artists George Catlin and Karl Bodmer.

BIRDS OF THE WORLD in Field and Garden combines colorful photographs and an informative text to describe some of the world's most interesting birds.

BUTTERFLIES AND MOTHS around the World describes the process by which a caterpillar becomes a butterfly or moth and presents the habits and characteristics of more than 50 species.

CREATURES OF POND AND POOL describes many of the beautiful and unusual creatures — frogs, water snakes, salamanders, aquatic insects — that live in and around fresh-water ponds.

DOMESTIC PETS describes the special characteristics of the animals which can live comfortably and happily with man, including several kinds of dogs, cats, birds, monkeys, reptiles, and fish.

WILD ANIMALS OF AFRICA takes the reader on a safari with German naturalist Klaus Paysan, who tells of his adventures in Africa and describes the living habits of the continent's most fascinating animals.

These fact-filled books contain more than fifty four-color plates and over 100 pages. Printed on high quality paper and reinforced bound, these books will add an exciting new dimension to any collection.

For more information about these and other quality books for young people, please write to

LERNER PUBLICATIONS COMPANY
241 First Avenue North, Minneapolis, Minnesota 55401

An Indian Policeman, an illustration from *Among the Plains Indians*